The Autobiography of Retired RUC Superintendent Tommy Reid

FROM THERE TO HERE

For Marie

Mother

and all my family

Tommy Reid was born in County Down in 1937, educated at Ballygowan P.E. School, Regent House Grammar School and later obtained a B.A. and B.Sc (Hons) degree at the Open University. He worked as an Office Boy, Iron Turner and Knitter before joining the R.U.C. in 1962 and served in South, North and West Belfast and in Newry and South Armagh throughout the terrorist campaign until his retirement in 1991. He was a keen sportsman having played Football, Rugby and Golf and enjoys music, being a proficient pianist and accordionist. On retirement, he acted as Honorary Secretary at his golf club for nine years.

Published by Thomas Reid
© Thomas Reid 2010

Designed by April Sky Design, Newtownards www.aprilsky.co.uk
Printed by Lulu.com

ISBN 978-0-9566830-0-7

April Sky Design
Jubilee Business Park
Jubilee Road
NEWTOWNARDS
County Down
Northern Ireland
BT23 4YH
Tel: 028 9182 6339
Fax: 028 9182 1900
E-mail: info@aprilsky.co.uk
Web-site: www.aprilsky.co.uk

The Autobiography of Retired RUC Superintendent Tommy Reid

FROM THERE TO HERE

Contents

Chapter 1
(Childhood and primary School)

I was born on the 19th May, 1937 in a nursing home in Comber Square, Co Down. Dr Wallace from Lisbane and Nurse McCartney attended at the birth. My father, Thomas James Reid was a lorry driver who worked for three uncles, the Miskelly Brothers, the owners of Miskelly's quarries in Ballygowan. My mother Mary Georgena Reid, came from farming stock and as well as being a hard-working housewife, also excelled at knitting and dress-making. They were both Presbyterians and politically inclined towards unionism, i.e.union with Britain, and supported the local Unionist party. I was eldest of three boys, my brother Robert Henry (Harry) three years younger and Wallace younger by seven years. My recollections are of a happy childhood although it was during the period of the 1939 – 1945 war and money was scarce. Food rationing was also very much in evidence and both parents worked hard to make ends meet. My earliest memories are when living at the Brae, Ballygowan, of my Uncle Bobbie, Bobbie Hunt and John Murray, two other friends of my father arriving at the house one night with pockets full of apples. They had raided an orchard belonging to James Frame, one of the publicans in the village, and I remember enjoying the apples and wondering at the antics of grown men acting like children.

Both parents were fond of music, my father sang in the church and male voice choirs and mother taught herself to play the violin and button keyed accordion. She had a lot of musical ability which unfortunately was not nurtured when she was a child. Many enjoyable nights were spent sitting around the fireside with only the glow of the fire and a few friends, mainly uncles, aunts and cousins, harmonising the popular war time songs just like the old barber shop quartets. Father's sister, Aunt Jeanie, was a beautiful singer and I can still hear her singing the spiritual 'How great thou art' in harmony with her great friend Eva Withers. These sessions probably fuelled my interest in music and I began to teach myself to play by ear an old piano belonging to Jacob Haire, the school Headmaster.

My first days as a four year old at Ballygowan Public Elementary School were a bit of an ordeal as I was shy and backward. I initially had a slight stammer which I later managed to control. The Headmaster, I knew well as he had been a friend of the family for a long time. However, the infant's class was taught by Miss Gibson who had the habit of sitting with her legs open, on a desk in front of the class with her feet on a chair, and after using her handkerchief, she deposited it up the leg of her knickers. She certainly got the attention of all the young boys. I have vague recollections of being unhappy in her class and running to the headmaster's class and holding on to his trousers while he was trying to teach the older pupils. However this must not have lasted too long as I continued with my primary education reasonably successfully. The school building owned by the Presbyterian Church, was a large imposing four storey building built with local stone. It had a tower with a clock, above which is written in large yellow lettering, 'THE TIME IS SHORT'. It was originally intended as a home for destitute children and named the 'Olivet Homes'. The school overlooked the village which was made up of the usual village square in which there were three pubs, Gourley's, Frame's and Murray's. Gourleys and Murrays also had grocery shops attached and Craigs butcher's shop and a post office also formed part of the businesses in the village. The Presbyterian Church is situated on a hill, about two hundred yards from the village, while the nearest Chapel is about five miles away in Carrickmannon. Most of the farmers in the outlying townlands did their shopping and socialising in Ballygowan. The years spent in the village were the happiest and most formative of my life. Summers were long and warm and I recall hard winters with plenty of snow.

I grew up with boundless energy and developed a love for football. Many happy hours were spent in the 'back field' behind the school, playing football both at lunch time and indeed many times after school. We never seemed to have time for meals as most of it was spent kicking a football. I had a good ear for music and my parents tried to nurture my interest by sending me to piano lessons in Belfast every Saturday morning. I travelled by bus to a Mr Stevenson in Jocelyn Avenue, off the Castlereagh Road. I got bored with trying to learn to read the music and used the money for lessons to go to the Castle cinema. It was some time before I was eventually caught out and the piano lessons stopped forthwith. One of my regrets in life is that I did not learn to read music properly having been given the chance to do so.

During our time in Ballygowan we had occasion to move house three times, firstly from the Brae, (where my brother Robert Henry (Harry) was born in 1940), to the school building on the side opposite the Headmaster's house. We replaced the Woods family who had moved to Ballygowan from Belfast during the war years and then moved back to Belfast. I had been friendly with Billy Woods and we were often chased by two huge Labrador dogs when we raided the orchard belonging to James Frame. Billy has since become famous for the treatment of leprosy when he became a missionary in Brazil. There were large rooms in the school building and I remember we had three lodgers, Tommy Gilmore, Ronnie Irvine and Miss Mercer, a teacher in Magherscouse School. She was good fun and one Christmas Eve when we were in bed, she dressed up as Santa and looked in at my brother Harry and I with a Santa mask and beard. We were both frightened out of our wits and hid beneath the sheets as we thought Santa had arrived early. On another occasion when we were playing hide and seek, I hid in the hot press in the bathroom and Miss Mercer came in and used the toilet. I really sweated for what seemed an eternity before she finally washed her hands and left.

Around this time, I began to experiment in smoking the odd cigarette. We were able to buy a cigarette and a match at Gourley's shop for a half penny and a pack of five Woodbine cigarettes cost twopence halfpenny, (About one penny in present money). My father was quite a heavy smoker and he ran out of cigarettes one Christmas Day when the shops of course were all closed. He was in a bad mood and when it started to snow, my brother Harry and I wanted out to play in the snow. He wouldn't let us out. I asked him if I could get him some cigarettes, would he let us out the play. He agreed so I went to the coal house in the yard where I had cigarettes stashed and took him ten woodbines. His face lit up in a huge smile for the first time that day and he asked me where I got them, but he kept his word and we got out to play in the snow.

My brother Wallace was born here in 1944 and I also have vivid memories of the celebrations and bonfires when the war ended in 1945. The Reverend McClarnon, our minister died when we lived there and a new minister, Reverend Stuart, replaced him. The church committee decided to update the Manse before the new clergyman moved in and they required the school house where we lived as a temporary residence for him, so we were compelled to move and share the house on the other side of the building with the school Headmaster, Jacob Haire for a short period. There was a grass tennis court just outside the front door and there were always a number of friends about playing tennis. I remember Doctor Wallace playing with my father and others and everyone enjoying the long summer evenings in the late nineteen forties.

Our third move was to a house just beside the quarry owned by Miskelly Brothers, my father's uncles. It was about a mile from the village and in the country. My brothers and I really enjoyed the open spaces and the three of us set up goal posts and had great fun playing football in the field adjoining the house. In the heat of the summer evenings, we often went across to the quarry where there was a huge pump hole filled with water about twenty feet deep and twenty feet across where we watched my father, a strong swimmer, dive in and enjoy a swim about. He was always nervous about us near deep water and forbid us to swim there. There was a peat bog in front of our house and we spent the long summer evenings playing Cowboys and Indians amongst the rocks and purple heather. We lived close to father's Uncle Tom and his wife Sarah who were childless. They grew very fond of my youngest brother Wallace, and he stayed with them a lot while my parents were working, father in the quarry and mother having a supervisor's job in a dress making factory in Belfast. I have memories of digging a hole in the peat moss and hiding my savings (seven shillings and sixpence) in an empty baked beans can, which was a small fortune to me in those days, then couldn't find it. It must still be there. Those were happy days with lots of fun and enjoyment, listening to the popular radio programmes, all the favourite songs of the day, the top twenty, on Radio Luxembourg and the popular detective drama at the time was "Dick Barton, Special Agent"!..

My grandmother on my mother's side, Georgena Bowman, lived with my Aunts, her children, Cissie, Carrie and Aggie in a farm on the Carrickmannon Road which was about a mile and a half from where we lived. Grandfather, Davy was a builder. The farm was about sixteen acres but he just let out the land and I remember him driving about the country in a Harley Davidson motor cycle and side car in which he carried his building materials and tools. He was known to have taken the short cut and driven against the one-way system on the Ballygowan roundabout at the junction of the Carrickmannon Road and Comber Road on many occasions. My Granny was a very happy- go -lucky person who enjoyed the company of children and would let us do anything we wished. My brother Harry and I would often walk to Grannie's house after school and she would bake soda bread on the large griddle which hung on the crook over the large open fire. The smell of the cooking bread was mouth watering and I have many happy memories of the 'craic' around the hearth, smoking cinnamon sticks. Davy would bring in the fiddle and I would learn the old Irish jigs and reels from him with the ridiculous names like, 'lizzie's the bugger for lick-in the sugar'. Davy had few teeth and he often tried to whistle the tunes to me so I could pick them up, but all I could hear was the rush of air. I also remember Martha Garrett arriving each Sunday on her bicycle with round portions of country butter which, when melted on the hot soda bread, really tasted delicious. Around that time, my Aunts were all young women and Cissie and Aggie were beginning to court. They didn't want two cheeky young boys hanging around when their boyfriends arrived. They often gave us a telling off but Granny always defended us. Aunt Carrie's nature was more laid back like Granny, and we got more sympathy from her. Later on in life when we were living in the city, my own children liked nothing better than to go to Granny Bowman's, play in the garden and sit around the large open fire listening to all the old stories and folk lore.

At about seven or eight years of age, I fell in love with a beautiful young girl who turned out to be the most important person in my life, Marie Brown. I was enraptured from the first time I saw her. I found she lived somewhere on the Ravara Road so I set out on my bicycle to find out exactly where. Once I knew where she lived, I began to try and see her at school as much as I could. I found after a while that apparently she had similar feelings towards me and many times after that, I would cycle to the Ravara Road in the mornings and have her to myself during the short journey to school. I must admit to being extremely jealous when any other boys would show an interest in Marie and I don't know how she put up with my petty jealousies in those days, but it does show that even at that tender age, we were capable of intense passions. I remember many times at variety concerts and Boys and Girls Brigade displays, we were continually looking out for each other and indeed at times we furtively held hands when we got near to each other during the shows and displays.

I became very depressed when Marie told me the family had

got a new house in Carrickmannon and she would have to move to Carrickmannon School. I implored her to stay at Ballygowan and she in fact pleaded with her parents to let her remain but it was not possible. When she moved, we lost touch for some time and I felt my world had come to an end. Sometimes, the Headmaster would require a message to be sent to Carrickmannon School and I would volunteer to ride the six miles on my bicycle in the hope of seeing Marie. This I managed on a couple of occasions but it was only a fleeting glance through a window. Marie however maintained her contact with Ballygowan through her Sunday School Class and through the church organisations such as the Girls Brigade so we began to get in touch again. The yearly Sunday school trip to Newcastle in the train was an another opportunity for me to be with Marie and we spent many happy hours

Later Newcastle trip.

in each others company exploring the amusements, climbing the Mournes and lying on the beach. Consequently, we celebrated fifty five happy years of marriage on 27th January, 2010.

My childhood years at Ballygowan School were about to come to an end when I sat the qualifying examination for the eleven plus. Only two of the senior class were entered for the examination, Nancy Gabbey and myself. We both managed to pass and were allocated places in Regent House Grammar School in Newtownards. The summer months in the year 1949 were spent messing about generally and playing football with my school friends and as we neared the start of the new school term in September, I was taken to the school clothing shops by mother and fitted out with the full regalia of navy blazer, grey flannels, navy burberry and red and black cap and badge which was required to keep up the standards of the Grammar School. In retrospect, the expense at this time on my parents must have been extreme but they were both proud that I had qualified and were determined to do their best for me.

Chapter 2
(Grammar School)

Travelling to Regent House Grammar School entailed a bus journey to Comber, then a change of bus onward to Newtownards. Pupils from the surrounding areas of Killinchy, Carrowdore , Ballywalter, Donaghadee, Millisle, Comber and Newtownards all congregated together at Regent House and the first few days at the school were very different to days at Ballygowan. The Headmaster at Regent House was James McDonald, a Comber man who was very interested in cricket, having played for North Down. The other sport was rugby and I think I immediately took a dislike to the school because there was no football being played. I believe I was intelligent enough to have done reasonably well but unfortunately did not have sufficient interest in subjects like French, Latin and English history which were being taught. The teachers at the school had great knowledge of their subjects and I particularly remember the Latin teacher, Ted Griffiths (a close friend of Blair Mayne of second world war notoriety, both past pupils of Regent House,) Ted had a great knowledge of Latin, but I did not apply myself so did not have the interest to retain the basics, and Ted, a decent mild mannered man, was not resolute enough to force or entice me into an attitude of interest or get the basics through to me. Consequently, I did not pay attention and when tests were carried out in mid term, I performed poorly in those subjects. I also found myself making friends with others who didn't have much interest in learning and we probably got the name of being rebels and so lived up to it.

The playing fields connected to Regent House were a good fifteen minutes walk from the school in Regent Street to the Comber Road. We often walked there to play rugby in the winter and cricket in the summer. I quite enjoyed playing rugby as I was fast and was selected to represent the School team regularly at Out Half or Fly Half as it was known then. We played the other well known Grammar Schools, Inst, Methodist College, R.B.A. Campbell College, Bangor Grammar and Wallace High in Lisburn and generally finished up around the middle of the league, winning some and losing more. On a couple of occasions during the walk to the sports fields in bad weather, another rebel, John McConnell and myself sneaked off into a cinema which we passed and instead of playing rugby in the cold and rain, we watched a good film in the warmth and comfort of the cinema. On one occasion, McConnell got involved with a girl sitting in front of us who was probably mitching from another school as well. He climbed over the seats to snog her and the next thing I knew, he hung her knickers over the back of the seat. I was mortified and cleared off to get my bus. We were eventually found out for missing training and paraded in front of the history class by the teacher Mr Stuart, who incidently had been an amateur boxer, and he punched us up and down the room until we were black and blue. Needless to say, we did not repeat the cinema trip.

Homework when one goes to a grammar school is an essential chore and I must admit that it was the last thing on my mind when I arrived home on the bus. Other interests such as music and football were much to the fore. As I now also played the accordion, I decided to form a band and play at country dances. I got together with Tom Dickson, a drummer and we started to play at the dancing class each Friday night in Moneyreagh Old School for twenty-five shillings each. While we were enjoying our interests, it was no picnic. There was no amplification equipment whatsoever. At times it was difficult even to hear the accordion music above the shouts and whoops of the dancers. Tom Savage, an old fiddler was purported to have stopped in the middle of a dance at Ardmillan and state to the dancers, "Yin mere hough and into the bagh she goes", meaning that if the noise and yelling of the dancers did not stop, he would put the fiddle in the bag and go home. The dances were mostly of the square dance variety such as the 'Lancers' and the 'Quadrilles'. There were also slow waltzes, quicksteps, 'pride of erin' waltzes and foxtrots thrown in for good measure. On every occasion, I left the dance with my left forearm aching from pulling the accordion bellows in and out, sometimes for a period of five hours or more. On one occasion when we played in the Orange Hall in Ballygowan, some people left the dance hall to catch the first bus to work at six o'clock in the morning. On reflection, it was hard earned pocket money. Other accordionists who had their own bands and I sometimes played with were, Jackie Savage, Will Craig, Everet McBride, Bobbie and Jim Geddis and Jimmy McVeigh. Another vivid memory was crowding into Jane Gibson's house in Ballygowan to watch the cup final at Wembley between Blackpool and Bolton. Jane had the only television in the village so most of the population was there.

Football also interfered with my schooling. I was football mad and in those days in Ballygowan, it was played with passion, especially the summer league. My father Tommy and Uncle Bobbie were useful footballers, both having played Irish First Division football, my father for Distillery and Bobbie for Cliftonville. Among my treasured possessions are gold medals won by my father, one for winning the Firth Cup while playing for Sirocco Works, the other an amateur league medal while playing for Killyleagh United. My football progressed from watching the Ballygowan team to playing in the school team then to the Ballygowan Youth team and to the Ballygowan full team. We won many competitions and I particularly remember playing in a match where the whole forward line of five players were related, myself, my father, my uncles Bobby Reid and Walter Frazer and a cousin, Bob Cunningham.

In those days it was played in the old fashioned way of goalkeeper, two full backs, three half-backs and five forwards, not the four, four two, or four, three, three so usual today. The emphasis was on

Ballygowan F.C. 1939

attack and I believe football in those days was a better spectacle to watch. There was fierce competition between teams from the different townlands such as Killinchy and Carrickmannon, each wanting to beat Ballygowan. At one Cup Final in Downpatrick, it took fourteen buses to carry the spectators to the away match.

Around this time, I was playing churches league and amateur league football with some Comber lads and I was asked to join the Army Cadet Corps in Comber who were organised and run by Mr Norman Nevan, the Secondary School master and Jack McGreehan, a civil servant. Mr Nevan had a great interest in youth football and picked a Northern Ireland Cadet side to play the Western Command at Goodison Park, Everton's ground. I remember the match and managed to score the winning goal when we won the first round of the knockout competition by defeating the Western Command Team by three goals to two. Mr Nevan was delighted and the next match was arranged against Northern Command to be played at Lincoln City's ground on the East Coast. We were confident and were a good footballing team. However, this match turned out to be more physical than we expected. They were a big strong lot and there was a lot of obstruction. They managed to prevent us from playing football. We were well beaten but were not used to so much obstructive play which the referee appeared to take little notice of. However we had a marvellous time and I enjoyed every minute. After my days in the cadets, I reverted to playing for Ballygowan in the summer league.

Between playing football, listening to Radio Luxemburg's top twenty and playing in a dance band, the writing was on the wall as far as my schooling was concerned. I was also friends with an

Ballygowan Y.F.C. 1952

older boy, Jim Meharry, a mechanic, who was a good friend of the School-master, Jacob Haire. Jim often borrowed an old 1937 maroon standard eight from the master and we could often be seen driving to Comber to the pictures, usually as fast as the old car would go. I can still remember the sound of the starter motor on that old car which sounded like a bell every time the starter button was pressed. On one of these trips to Comber, Jim met a girl called Irene Hiles who had a companion, Phylis Bennett. Jim started to go steady with Irene and as I went along with him, I felt I should at least make an effort to go out with Phylis who was slightly older than me. However, this didn't last long as I still was too interested in my first love, Marie, even though she had moved house to Carrickmannon. Marie eventually got a job in Ballygowan post office so I was able to see her more often. After a long relationship, Jim and Irene eventually got married.

The Junior Certificate examinations were approaching at Regent House and after three years of unproductive study, I was completely at odds with the school. I recall, the Headmaster, Mr McDonald who obviously had monitored my lack of progress saying to me in front of my friends, "I take it Reid, you will not be coming back to Regent House after the Junior Certificate examinations"?, and I immediately replied, " No. You are quite correct. I definitely will not." He strutted off in anger and my friends were open mouthed in amazement that I had answered him so abruptly. I was fed up and did poorly in the exams because of my inattention to basics in the first year and because homework had taken a back seat to all my other interests. I decided to leave school and managed to convince my parents there was no point continuing at Regent House.

Chapter 3
(Work)

My first job was as an office boy with David Marshall & Son, a lorry retailer in Bedford Street, Belfast. I worked in the office with a Miss Williams, (a bullying, bossy, middle aged, chain smoking spinster with a dry sense of humour who I eventually grew to like) learning how to do invoices, receipts and dealing with the income tax, national insurance etc, for the pay of the twenty or so employees. However, I spent most of my time running messages for Miss Williams and didn't learn an awful lot. There was nothing much in the business in the way of prospects to hold my interest so I decided after six months that I would serve my time to a trade. I got a job as an apprentice iron turner with John Hind & Son at Prince Regent Road, Castlereagh and travelled to work each day with Sam Kerr, who was an old school colleague and who also worked in the firm as a fitter. There was an atmosphere of hustle and bustle around the factory which employed about thirty men of all ages and characters. I quite enjoyed my time at the factory but after three years of trying to become a competent iron turner, (which I don't think I would have accomplished), my circumstances changed dramatically and I had to consider taking a job that would bring in more income than an apprentice iron turner. However, I was still playing football for Ballygowan in the Killyleagh summer league and also for Hearts in the Cardy League in the Newtownards area.

I was still seeing the love of my life, Marie. We were very much in love and were together at every opportunity. Marie's Mum and Dad went to the boxing at the Ulster Hall every Saturday night and I, together with Jim Douglas who was courting Marie's sister Margaret, went up to their house in Carrickmannon in Jim's old standard car. We began to go out together seriously and Marie came to some of the dances that I played at, although she didn't dance and was probably uncomfortable sitting on her own while I was on stage playing the accordion. Marie also came to see me playing football in the summer league and remembers standing up for me when anyone criticised my playing abilities. We were both young, very much in love and neither of us had much experience in sexual matters. It was a shock to both of us when Marie told me she was with child, although in retrospect, it was inevitable. We were never in any doubt that we wanted to spend the rest of our lives together so we told our parents and were married on 27th January, 1955 at a quiet ceremony in Carrickmannon. Photographs were taken at Farnum Nixon's house in Killinchy. Marie's parents, George and Sarah moved to Comber and we stayed with them for a short period before finding a flat of our own at 76a Dunsy Way in Comber.

My job as an apprentice iron turner did not bring in sufficient money to keep a family so I applied for a job as a knitter at Berkshire Nylon Factory in Newtownards. This improved our income a lot and when my daughter Valerie was born in July, 1955 we were in a much better financial position. Nevertheless, I will be forever grateful to my own, and Marie's parents George and Sarah for helping us through a most difficult period. I continued to play football in those days and while my life probably did not change much, Marie was a first class wife and mother, and held the family together. My daughter Gwendoline, was born in September, 1956 and in my spare time, I was still played the accordion and piano at dances with the Metro Dance Band at Crossgar Memorial Hall and later with Roy McCord and his band at Greyabbey Hall and throughout the Ards peninsula. The extra money was useful as my family increased, Marie was generally at home looking after the children and in retrospect, there is no doubt that she was the rock which kept the family together as I was not always available to accept my share of parenting responsibilities.

I did however continue to work hard at Berkshire Nylon factory in Newtownards. This was an American firm making nylon stockings and the factory ran on a twenty four hour basis, three shifts of eight hours changing each week, seven in the morning to three in the afternoon, three in the afternoon to eleven in the evening and night shift from eleven in the evening until seven in the morning. Initially I had no transport so I rode a bicycle the four miles from Comber to Newtownards each shift and I remember travelling home from work on an evening shift, a policeman stopped me and summonsed me for having no rear light on my bicycle. I went to the Court in Newtownards and explained to the resident Magistrate, Mr John Long, that as far as I was concerned the light had gone out without my knowledge. He asked me where I lived and when he found out that I was riding from Comber to Newtownards to work he fined me one shilling. I began to get a lift with a Scotsman, Jock who lived close to me and had a Triumph Tiger 100 motor cycle. I never felt safe riding pillion to Jock as I didn't rate his driving and eventually managed to buy an N.S.U. Quickly, a motorised version of a bicycle and I thought I was in heaven not having to push the bicycle the five miles to and from work. I later traded it in for a 250 Royal Enfield Clipper motorcycle which I enjoyed very much until the front wheel slipped in the snow in Newtownards square into the path of an on-coming car. Luckily, the car had time to stop but I recognised the danger and sold the motor bike. It was about this time I decided to get a dog and bought an Alsatian which we called Sabre. He became a real pet but he never could get used to postmen and while we enjoyed having him, we were always worried in case he would savage one of them.

Tragedy struck the family on 14th August, 1957. Marie's brother Bobbie was walking home from Crossgar to Kilmore one evening when he came across an Ulster Special Constabulary patrol checking vehicles on the road. He stopped to talk to one of the special constables known to him and after some comment during the conversation, the constable raised his hand to toss

Bobbie's hair. He had a sten gun hanging from his shoulder and one of his tunic buttons caught the trigger as he lifted his arm. As the gun was on automatic fire, two shots were discharged and entered Bobbie's heart, killing him instantly. This tragedy was similar to that of my own grandfather on my Father's side who while travelling in the back seat of a car driven by my uncle near the police training depot in Newtownards in the early nineteen twenties, was shot dead when a police patrol fired through the rear window of the car when it failed to stop. My uncle had not seen the signal. This was before I was born and my Grandmother Rose and my father had great difficulty in coming to terms with it.

When Marie and I heard the bad news about Bobbie, we immediately arranged to have our children looked after and went to console firstly Marie's mother and father George and Sarah, then Bobbie's wife, Sadie. Their little girl, Alexander was too young to realise what had happened. Bobbie was well known and friends came from far and near to pay their respects. The large funeral from their house in Kilmore to the cementary in Derryboy Road, Crossgar, was a sad affair and the Special Constable who was involved was inconsolable. Marie's mother was also heart broken but to her credit spoke to the man concerned and told him she realised it was a complete accident and she bore him no ill-feeling. However, she was never the same woman after Bobbie's death.

While at Berkshire, football was still a big part of my life and I was asked to play for the Berkshire Football team. In the 1957 – 58 season we won the Cardy Cup, beating Portavogie in the final at Castlereagh Park by five goals to two. I was fortunate to score two goals in that match. I also played for Tower United and when we won the Gibson Cup, I got two goals in the final against Belfast City Hospitals. Hearts was another team I played for in the Cardy summer league together with Terry Gillespie and Jim Murphy, two colleagues whom I had played with in the amateur league for Comber Rec and with Ballygowan in the summer league. Hearts won the league having scored twenty two points

Berkshire FC 1958

out of a possible twenty four and I will always remember Ronnie Burns who played inside me on the left wing as an excellent and intelligent inside forward who made scoring easy for me on many occasions. He reminded me of Sammy Smyth of Wolverhampton Wanderers and Irish International fame who I was to meet later, and Ronnie was a player who if around today and had the proper level of fitness, could be in one of the top teams in the premier league. I also played a few matches for Ards Town.

My brothers Harry and Wallace were both good footballers, probably as a result of so much football in the fields behind the house. Harry was a very strong half back and Wallace an inside forward. Harry would have made a name for himself in football but he became more interested in religion which took over from his passion for football. He began to see a girl, Jean Rutherford, who had similar interests, and it was no surprise when he and Jean decided to get married and set out to the mission fields in Brazil where for many years, they carried out excellent work. They still travel to Brazil on a yearly basis. Wallace on the other hand was playing regularly for Newtownards Technical College and to such a standard that he was selected to play for the Northern Ireland Schools International Team in the Victory Shield match against Scotland at Grosvenor Park on 19th March, 1960. The Irish team beat Scotland by four goals to three and Wallace had an excellent game at inside left. He further represented the Northern Irish Schools against England at York City's ground the following week but they were beaten by four goals to one by a very strong English side.

His third Schools International Cap came against Wales at Swansea on 19th April, 1960 and as a result of his performances, he was approached by a Newcastle scout and signed apprentice professional forms for Newcastle United. He asked the scout, Matt Willis, if he could also take his friend David Craig with him. The scout agreed to go and see David play in a Boys Brigade match and then said he would also take him. Both went to Newcastle but after a year or so, Wallace became homesick and left. David stayed and represented Newcastle United and indeed Northern Ireland on many occasions. I do remember my parents receiving a letter from the late great Ivor Allchurch, a Welsh International, who was on the coaching staff at Newcastle pleading with them to persuade Wallace to come back to Newcastle as he was capable of playing International football and had the talent to be a star of the future.

Wallace signed Amateur forms for Linfield and while with them, acquired three Youth International caps. Against Scotland, on 23rd April, 1963, whom they beat by two goals to one, the great Pat Jennings was in goal but Pat signed professional forms for Watford and so became ineligible for the next two matches against England at Boundary Park, Oldham, and Wales at Aberystwyth. Both these matches played on May 11th and May 18th 1963 respectively, were drawn one goal each, and Wallace partnered the legendary George Best in each of these on the left wing, which was reported as a good partnership. He then worked as a draughtsman in Short and Harland's and after short spells with Distillery and

Larne, like his brother Harry, began to take a close interest in religious matters. He met Molly, his present wife, and when their children Stephen, Ian and Paul were born, they became involved with the missions and decided to emigrate to Australia. Wallace is now a pastor of the Emmanuel Baptist Church in Sydney and until recently, still enjoyed playing football with his sons.

Football in Ballygowan brought Protestants and Catholics together. It was unfortunate that during school years, both religions were educated separately, mainly through the Catholic Church's need to maintain their identity and control. There were also difficulties in our protestant education in that we were taught very little of Irish history, everything was British orientated, hence, while we were children, there was the Catholic School, St Marys at Burns Cross and our School, Ballygowan Public Elementary, a case of them and us, with very little social interaction at that crucial stage. I remember walking to school at Ballygowan and the Catholic children walking to Burns Cross. We met on opposite sides of the road and passed each other with suspicious glares, thinking we were different. It was only in our teens that social intercourse through football began and while there may have been some who always harboured feelings of distrust for each other, I had no hang ups and always took people as I found them.

I had great friends in Roland Adair, Jim Peake, Micky McMahon, Alex McMahon and Charlie McCartney who were all good footballers and all Catholics. We played together, supported together and lived in harmony throughout the summer months. There was great camaraderie and no animosity whatsoever between players of different religions. However, around the 12th July each year feelings in the village began to get a little edgy. The 12th Day itself was not a problem as many of the Catholic neighbours came out to listen to the bands and watch the Orangemen setting out to the field, but I do have memories of the 11th night celebrations where bonfires were lit and emotions were fuelled by the intake of intoxicating liquor. This sometimes led to impromptu bands being formed and marching with drums beating past a Catholic Row of houses in a triumphalist fashion playing Protestant songs such as the Sash my Father Wore and Derry's Walls. As a young person, I probably did not realise the effect this behaviour had on our Catholic neighbours but as I grew older and more aware, I began to see this bit of coat-trailing was distasteful and uncalled for, but it was confined to one night of the year and didn't appear to effect relationships unduly. It was generally ignored by the Catholic population.

The 'live and let live' attitudes between the religions at that time was also due in no small way to two men, the Catholic priest, the late Father Shields and the protestant clergyman, the late Rev, McClarnon. These men maintained a friendship, led by example, were highly respected in all areas and worked together unceasingly to promote good relations. This was in stark contrast to the attitudes of some senior clergy from both religions, I later encountered in my police service. In those days, the main persons in the village who everyone in the community looked up to were the minister or priest, the doctor and the schoolmaster. Each denomination was very much church, school and family oriented and thus a measure of control was maintained over young people who were brought up to show respect to their elders. Hence the generally good relations between the religions at the summer league football matches.

It was during the summer league matches that my progress as a footballer caught the eye of George Eastham Senior, a former English International, who at that time managed Ards in the Irish League. He came to a match and afterwards asked me to sign for Ards. I found him to be a gentleman and he gave me personal coaching during training sessions at the Ards ground, concentrating on making me kick with my right foot as I was very much left sided. I played a few matches for Ards second eleven but I found it difficult to fit in with the established team members who were in a clique and probably saw me as a threat to their positions.

I played a few times with George Eastham (jun) who also later became an English International, but at the time, although he had excellent ball control and technical ability, I considered him to be a selfish player who took too much out of the ball. I felt he often held the ball too long, brought it towards his winger and only passed it when he could do nothing more with it. This brought the opposing defence across to the left and the winger was generally by this time trapped in the corner. He was very young at the time and later developed into a brilliant player who represented his country on many occasions.

I signed for Bangor the following year together with Micky McMahon. Jack Gaw was chairman and I was approached by Dicky Horner and Sammy Smyth already mentioned, who had been a Northern Irish International and an inside forward with Wolverhampton Wanderers. He was player manager at Bangor at the time. I had the privilege of playing alongside him in the warm up matches at the start of the season. He was a great player even in the twilight of his career and had the ability to make a left winger look good. He often gathered the ball in midfield, wandered towards the right, taking the opposing defence with him then suddenly change direction and flash a slide rule pass to the left wing. On many occasions I just had to run on to the ball and shoot to score. I really enjoyed my time at Bangor while Sammy was manager but he resigned after an altercation with the committee over dropping a centre forward, Johnny Neilson from the first team. Johnny refused to play in the reserve team and the committee failed to back Sammy's decision to play him in the reserves. Unfortunately, Sammy's leaving was a great loss of experience and know- how to Irish football at that time. I lost interest in senior football and decided I would better enjoy football in the Amateur divisions.

I had many happy footballing moments with Ballygowan in the summer league, Comber Rec and Tower United in the amateur league, Hearts, Berkshire and Cardy Rovers in the Cardy league

31

Cardy Rovers F.C. 1960

and finally with the R.U.C. in the amateur league.

Meantime, my work at Berkshire had become monotonous and after seven years, although the money was good, I was unsettled. There was an I.R.A. terrorist campaign taking place between 1955/1956 and I thought at that time I would like to join the police force. My father had been a member of the Ulster Special Constabulary from 1939 until 1955. This entailed going out on patrol during the war years on a voluntary basis and assisting the local police with road stops etc and on one occasion in the 1940's when German prisoners who were being held at Ballykinlar escaped, the USC assisted in capturing and returning them to the prison camp. The USC as I knew them in Ballygowan were a dedicated band of decent men who gave of their time mainly voluntary to support law and order, not the bigoted anti catholic force as later portrayed by the massive IRA propaganda machine. While any large organisation will have bigots, particularly understandable in the confrontational interface areas in Belfast, my perception is that the large majority of the USC were decent working men who were mainly trying to uphold law and order and their Unionist tradition. In retrospect, there is no doubt that these simple hard-working men were used by the ruling classes who were intent on maintaining the unionist political majority.

I thought I would like to do my share in the protection of the Unionist and British way of life in our country. I went to Comber Police Station in 1956 and put in an application with Sergeant Barker to join the R.U.C. However, at that time, the Sergeant was the recruiting officer and this would have meant a lot of work for him. He convinced me that as my height was on the lower limit, five foot nine and a half inches, that my application would be unlikely to succeed with the result that I withdrew my application. My daughter Gwendoline was born on 21st September, 1956, and in the same year, the IRA campaign in Ulster lost momentum and fizzled out through lack of support from the Catholic community. Our third daughter, Carol Sally was born on 12th December, 1960, so with three children and an Alsatian to keep, I could not do anything foolish like leave my job before I had found another, so I continued to work at the Berkshire factory, even though I had lost interest and had little motivation.

For the next two years, I still retained the dream to join the police force and this was known by my father in law, George. He knew a District Inspector at that time called Ross McGimpsey and mentioned it to him. He sent word to me through my father in law to apply again at Comber and this time my application was accepted and I was called to County Headquarters at Downpatrick for a selection board and a medical examination. Shortly after that, a letter arrived that I had been selected as a recruit for the Royal Ulster Constabulary. Training at the Depot in Enniskillen lasted for a period of six months and this created a problem. My Alsatian, Sabre, was a large dog who needed plenty of daily exercise which I had been able to provide, both by taking him for long walks and taking him with me on shooting trips across the fields. It would have been unfair to leave that chore to Marie as she had to look after the three children so I decided to get him a good home. A colleague from Berkshire wanted an Alsatian so I let him go. I was later disappointed to learn that he didn't settle and ended up with a security firm.

Chapter 4
(The Depot)

On 5th November, 1962, I kissed Marie and the children good-bye and headed off to Enniskillen with my bags packed. At the time, we owned a green 1950 Citroen light Fifteen and I drove to the depot with mixed feelings of anticipation and excitement. I was now twenty six years of age, had a wife and three children, finally felt I had found my vocation in life and was determined to make the most of it. First impressions were a bit intimidating as there was a squad of about twenty four recruits being drilled and the bark of the instructor's voice rang across the parade ground. I met other recruits and noticed they were all taller and younger than I. We were shown to a dormitory and began to converse and make friends. There was so much to do, uniforms were issued, boots and books required to be purchased at the depot shop, cost of which were taken from our first pay which was now monthly and wasn't due until 30th of the month. This was difficult as I had been used with a weekly income so was not able to send anything home for four weeks. When the pay did come, (about £28 with all the deductions), I had to send it all home to Marie. I had been earning nearly this amount each week at Berkshire. At that stage, I wondered if I had made a mistake but decided to continue. Marie had of necessity to take up employment in Comber to make ends meet. Unfortunately, this was short lived as she injured her foot on a kerb while making her way to answer a telephone call I made from the depot and was unable to continue to work.

Squads were given a consecutive letter of the alphabet as they arrived and I was appointed to "H" squad. It was unusual in that it comprised of fourteen men and fourteen women. It was the first mixed gender squad for some time so created some interest from the other four all male squads already in training. There was a tradition that the squads already in training performed an initiation ceremony on new recruits shortly after they arrived. This consisted of manhandling each recruit naked into a cold bath and black balling them with boot polish around the genitals. Some recruits took this better than others and some fought back but generally to no avail. I should point out that this ceremony only took place with the male students, the females in the squad were untouched. Once this initiation was dispensed with, everyone was made welcome and there was great camaraderie between the squads. It was known that I had an interest in football and I was chosen to play for the depot football team.

At that time, in one of the senior squads, there was a recruit from the Middle East who was a member of the ruling family in Bahrain. He was sent to the Royal Ulster Constabulary training school because of the excellent nature of the training and was destined to go to Sandhurst Military Academy in England after his training in the depot, probably to give him a good insight into the disciplines necessary in preparation to rule a country. His name was Isa Bin Ahmed Al Kalifa and he was a lovely quiet natured lad who easily integrated into depot life and took all the banter thrown at him and gave as much as he received. He also loved football and was a really good half back. He was nicknamed "The Sheik" and also played for the Depot football team at left half behind me when I played on the left wing. We were all reasonably fit through all the training at the depot and I was selected for the R.U.C representative team which played in the amateur league. This meant that I was able to travel to Belfast each week end to play football, spend the week-end at home with Marie and the kids and travel back to Enniskillen on Sunday evenings. I was the envy of the rest of the squad who only got home a couple of times in six months.

The Sergeant responsible for the drilling of our squad was Victor Dobbin, an ex Irishguards' man with a posture as straight as a ramrod. The first day we assembled in the drill square, he must have thought, "how am I going to sort out this lot?" Spencer

Cusack and I were the smallest at 5' 9 1/2" and the other extreme was Willie John Holmes at 6' 5". Between these two extremes there were a number of queer looking individuals, men and women who looked nothing like a drill squad. However, Sergeant Dobbin began to try and whip us into some sort of a shape which would pass for a drill squad on the passing out parade in six months time. There was about an hour of drill each morning when we would be shown how to march, turn left and right and about, stand at ease and attention, slope and order arms. The remainder of the time would be spent in school, learning definitions and all current law. There were also fitness classes and road runs throughout the week.

Despite the difficulties we had in drilling, we began to take a great personal pride in what we were trying to do and ever person gave it their best shot. There is no doubt that the amount of work each day, which included, learning definitions, learning law, spit and polishing our boots, by firstly burning them with a candle, then spitting and polishing until the toe-caps were shining like a mirror, gave little time for socialising but we still managed to enjoy ourselves. We were allowed out on the town now and again on a limited basis and because of my position as a married man with three children, I had to send all of my money back to Marie to keep things going at home. My socialising consisted of a night out with my mates at the Central Bar in Enniskillen where they bought a drink and I played the piano for the remainder of the evening and was plied with drinks by the patrons. Very often, when I was off playing football at the weekends, my colleagues informed me that the bar manager would ask, "where is the rookie piano player tonight?".

Examinations were held every so often to test how we were progressing in our knowledge of police law and I did reasonably well in most of them, mainly because I was well motivated in that I was now twenty six years of age and intended to make a career out of the police. I also obtained a first and second class certificate of education at the depot which was essential to progress to Sergeant or Head constable rank in the force. I had more experience of life than many of the younger recruits and I was determined to make a go of it. However, during a football match playing for the R.U.C. representative side against Comber Recreation, a team that I used to play for, on a freezing Saturday in February, 1963, I was running through with a chance to score when the goalkeeper dived out over the ball and I took his full weight through his shoulder on my left shin. I think I got the ball past him to score but there was this almighty crack when both ankle bones, tibia and fibula, were broken. My brother Harry was on his way to the match and he was about three hundred yards away when he heard the crack. I knew immediately what had happened and the shock and cold made me shiver violently. I was lying on my right side and my left foot was pointing left at 180 degrees. I heard someone say, "get him to his feet" and I shouted 'my bloody leg is broken, leave me'!. I was eventually taken to Newtownards Hospital where I spent the next six months and five operations which ended with a plate being inserted before I returned to the depot. One memory which stays with me is that a senior officer, a County Inspector, had been sent from Headquarters to see me and inform me even though I was representing the Royal Ulster Constabulary, "Reid, you know you were not on duty when this injury occurred." This gave me an insight into the mentality of some of the assholes who were in charge of the R.U.C. at the time, afraid that I might claim compensation.

Notwithstanding, I cannot speak highly enough for the persons in charge of the R.U.C. football team. The late Davy Watton and the late Dennis Maloney called to see me without fail every week for the six months I remained in hospital and the Instructors from the depot in Enniskillen did their best for me when I returned on crutches. I had been told that my left leg would have been two inches shorter had I not had the plate fitted, so my career as a police officer was certainly in the balance. The Commandant of the Depot, Tom Crozier, remarked once that I was not yet out of the woods when I was going to class using my crutches and the late Sergeant John Tourney, one of the instructors, took my crutches from me one morning when the rest of the squad were preparing for a road run and made me run around the running track at the depot when I could hardly walk. I was still in great pain and called him a great bastard at the time but later realised he was trying to ensure I finished my training and end up as a fully fledged policeman. Another instructor to whom I owe a lot was Jack McFarland who got me to the swimming pool at Portora

N Squad
1963

Grammar School as often as possible to strengthen my leg. Both John Tourney and Jack McFarland were ex Royal Marines and I really appreciate what they did for me. Unfortunately, John Tourney was later to shoot himself following a stupid drunken escapade at a local golf club.

Because of the time in hospital, my original squad had finished their training and had passed out to their driving course. I also lost touch with Isa Kalifa, "The Sheik", who had moved on to Sandhurst. I was allocated a place in "N" squad, an all male squad and had to make friends all over again as they were only about one month into their training. The first two men to make friends were Willie Martin and Jimmy Robertson. Jimmy was a County Fermanagh man from Fivemiletown and Willie was from Limavady and had played for Limavady United at soccer and so we had something in common. Jimmy had a great sense of humour and we had many a laugh. My car at that time had been lying at Enniskillen over the whole of the freezing winter and the engine had frozen up. It was useless to me in that condition so I sold it to Bob Harper, a constable at the local station for £15. I was later to serve with Bob at Willowfield Station in Belfast. Jimmy Robertson was driving a beautiful blue Vauxhall Velox at that time and he loaned it to me to travel home when I had weekend leave. This was very much appreciated by both Marie and I, otherwise, I would have been unable to travel. Unfortunately, Jimmy who had been a bread server in county Fermanagh prior to joining the police, a virtually crime free county, found it very difficult to apply the law to people he had known for years and decided the police service was not for him. He ended up a successful businessman in Fivemiletown.

The intricacies of learning the law continued unabated at the Depot. The fact that the arrest of a person in which you deprive him/her of their liberty was completely the last resort was hammered into us at every opportunity and that it was imperative that evidence was obtained before and not after arrest. The present day situation appears to fly in the face of all that we were taught at the depot and what I consider to be this most important procedure as we constantly hear of arrests immediately after a crime has been committed, obviously without evidence as the suspects are subsequently released without charge to give the impression that situations are under control when there is insufficient evidence. The fact that all persons should be treated with courtesy and good temper was also drummed into us in training and I found on many later occasions that these rules enabled me to defuse many situations in my capacity as a police officer. When I look back on those days and despite the propaganda of the terrorist organisations to the contrary over the last thirty years, the training of the Royal Ulster Constabulary leading up to the troubles in the 1960's was of the highest standards. It is unfortunate that because of the continuous threat of terrorist activity, the paramilitary nature of the training was essential.

After six months hard work in school work and physical training, the day of the passing out parade finally arrived. Many hours were spent on preparation of uniforms and spit and polish on boots until the shine on the toe caps reflected everything within range. The R.U.C. band arrived early on the day and the rousing sounds of the march, the Old May Moon, the signature tune of the Royal Ulster Constabulary, echoed around the parade ground. This tune still fills me with pride and brings me to the brink of tears when I think of the sacrifices that so many of my colleagues made as does one of the marches of the Ulster Defence Regiment, Killaloo. We marched proudly through the passing out ceremony, all realising that we had acquired much more self esteem than when we arrived at the depot. We felt part of a large family on which the future of our country depended. I feel that every person in that passing out parade, protestant and catholic, will remember the occasion with pride. It was an emotional time when we had to leave after having spent so much time together as each of us was destined to go to different places in Northern Ireland. We said our goodbyes and my first assignment was to a driving course at Musgrave Street station where I spent three weeks on the course and assessed to drive police cars. Sergeant Fieldie Robinson was my driving instructor and somehow I was passed to be a police driver.

Chapter 5
(Willowfield)

My first station was Willowfield R.U.C. Station in East Belfast. On arrival, I was met by the station sergeant Jack Creagmile who lived in the station house attached to the police station. The sergeant, a devoted Christian, made me feel very welcome and the senior men at the station all having many years of experience looked after me and kept me on the right track. I particularly remember Leslie Taylor, Tommy Graham, Brendan Hopkins, John Neilly and Ted Storey, a former boxer who had boxed for the R.U.C. The younger men at the station were also very friendly and special friends were Brian Blacker, Bob Harper and John Craig. The supervising Sergeants were, Joe McClelland, {big Joe} and Davy Bell { Dinger}. Joe McClelland was a very intelligent person who because of his rebellious attitude and inclination to speak his mind, had probably been overlooked for promotion to Head Constable. The Head Constable at Willowfield was Bob Nixon, also a very decent man who took an interest in how new recruits were settled in. He was unfortunately to drop dead in the Station yard after suffering a massive heart attack. He was replaced by Head Constable Herbie Hutchinson who moved in from Fermanagh and who was also a very decent policeman with loads of common sense.

Another character in the division was the district motor cyclist, Davy McKirgan, who through his love for golf and his sense of humour, became a very close friend. Davy had been promoted on a couple of occasions but when he went to his allocated station, he was left to work out pay-sheets etc on his own, having had no previous experience in such office work, On each occasion, he asked to be reverted to constable and his request was granted and he returned to the Willowfield area. One amusing story occurred when Davy was sent out on duty by the Sergeant when he served in a country station. When Davy found the British Open Golf Championship was to be held at Portrush in 1951, he managed to wangle a turn at tillage duty on that day. This was duty in which you called at all the farms in the district and did a tillage census. The night before, he planted his Francis Barnett motor cycle at one of the farms and the next morning, left the station to do the tillage duty. He arrived at the said farm, pulled a civvy coat on over his uniform and headed to Portrush on his motor bike. That evening, the Sergeant and others in the station were watching the climax of the golf as the winner, Max Faulkner, was walking down the eighteenth fairway on their black and white T.V. Who should appear walking behind Faulkner as bold as brass and soaking up the atmosphere but the bold Davy McKirgan. You can imagine the dialogue between the Sergeant and Davy when he arrived for duty the following morning.

Davy got the name of being a tight fisted individual and so lived up to it in a 'tongue in cheek' type of way. He was always the last to buy a drink and the story was that he cancelled the milk when he was on night duty because he cadged a bottle from the early morning milkman. On one occasion, we were playing golf at his club, Portstewart, and as I was walking down a fairway, I looked across and Davy was lying flat out on his face on the fairway. I thought he had collapsed and ran across to him to see if he was alright. Apparently there was a rabbit hole on the fairway into which golf balls would occasionally run and he was checking to see if he could find any. I was also in the car with him when he switched off the engine to save petrol when going down hills.

Meanwhile, I was working in Belfast and it was important that the family were within a reasonable distance so Marie and I began looking for a suitable house nearer to Willowfield Station. We viewed a house in Kilbroney Bend in the Cregagh Estate and decided to move there. This meant uprooting our children from Comber School and re-locating them at Cregagh. Valerie and Gwendoline had made friends in Comber but it was not long before they had integrated into the Cregagh environment. Carol was still very young and when she eventually reached school age, she moved into the school with her sisters. We had good neighbours, Mr & Mrs Vincent Jamison on our right and Mr & Mrs Kennedy on our left, both catholic families. Kilbroney Bend in Cregagh was on the opposite side of a green where George Best lived and often played as a boy and my daughters went to school and played netball with his sister Barbara. It was about one mile from Willowfield Station along the Cregagh Road in a mainly protestant working class area. There were quite a number of Catholic families in the area around the chapel not far from the police station who felt reasonably secure in the early sixties as there were no great problems. I knew one particular family called Murray from Ballygowan, my home village, and I called regularly when on the beat.

The Willowfield police area at that time covered a large area, from Ladas Drive to the Albertbridge Road and including the Ravenhill Road, Cregagh Road Woodstock Road and as far across as the Bloomfield Road. For patrol purposes, it was divided into beats, One, Two and Three. The population, around forty thousand, was mainly working class and the further you moved from the city centre, tended to contain more elderly people. Subsequently, there was a high rate of sudden deaths to be dealt with as well as the usual police work, of thefts, motor accidents, house-breaking, assaults, licencing laws, indecencies and so on. I attended many of the sudden deaths and indeed the post-mortems following the deaths. Probably because I had shown some interest in what the pathologist was doing to find the cause of death, I feel the then pathologist, an Indian gentleman, actually asked for me to be present at the post-mortems as I seemed to get more than my fair share.

There was a man called Lavery who lived alone in Mount Street and was continually in jail. He used to break into his gas meter, then give himself up to police, probably to get back to jail to the company. I was required to take him to court and the prosecutor was Head Constable Issac Keiltley, a very large man who smoked cigars. He also had a very wide girth and cigar ash was continually falling on the front of his uniform. He got into a habit of brushing the front of his tunic with his hands while prosecuting. Issac was brushing away at his tunic when the case came up and he addressed the Magistrate with the words, "Your worship, this man is a professional Corporation Safe-breaker;" The magistrate, Jerry Lynn, almost fell out of his seat with laughter. We had a report of a young fellow exposing himself to young female workers on the Cregagh Road and arrangements were made for one of our senior female officers to patrol in plain clothes. Sure enough, the next morning he was there and exposed himself to Jean who arrested him and told him to come back and show it to her 'when it grows'.

Two accidents I dealt with as a young constable stick out in my mind, one happened at John Long's corner on a quiet Sunday afternoon when a young pregnant wife was trying to cross the road when a motor scooter driven by a youth knocked her down. I was on the beat and came on the scene immediately and got her conveyed to hospital. She died in hospital and her unborn child was taken from her but also died after two weeks. This was my first experience of breaking bad news to a family and I will always remember the heartache felt at that time. Unfortunately, this was to be the first of many times, I was the bearer of bad tidings.

I was on the beat in Cregagh Road when the second accident referred to occurred. There was heavy traffic and I saw an elderly woman walking straight out into the roadway in front of me without even lifting her head to look. She walked in front of a young motor cyclist who was travelling in traffic at a normal speed and he swerved violently to avoid her, causing him to fall off his machine into the path of an oncoming car. He fell beneath the front wheel and died a short time later in hospital. It transpired he was the son of the headmaster, Mr Cuddy of Park Parade School whom I knew well. I was again required to go to the family and break the bad news. Again, a twenty one year old young man who had done nothing wrong was dead. It is difficult to erase these events from ones mind and indeed the images are always with me as I was required to attend the post mortems on these young bodies to ascertain the exact cause of death.

There were many happy times at Willowfield Station in the sixties. Most of the constables had their calling houses on each beat where they could slip in for a cup of tea and a quick chat. The publicans were also glad to see you coming in after closing time so they could get the place cleared and there was always a bottle of stout for the constables after the punters had been cleared out. The station personnel got on very well together and looked after each others interests. At weekends, at the bottom of the Woodstock Road, a mainly Protestant area, when the locals had a few more drinks than usual, there would be some trouble. It bordered with the Catholic Short Strand so there was always the underlying sectarian tension. On a Friday and Saturday night, rather than one man on the beat, it was doubled to two men. Mitchel's dance hall at the bottom of the Woodstock Road had to be supervised as fights often occurred there. The senior men were adept in handling a rowdy situation and nine times out of ten, were able to diffuse a situation by persuasion rather than using the heavy hand. This was born out of a great local knowledge, not only of the area, but on the temperament of the people. The 'hards' were more easy to deal with when they knew you knew who they were. In time, I managed to build up a very good local knowledge of the residents in each beat and I also had my calling houses for tea and biscuits.

Favourite calling places in Willowfield's police area were Meg Wallace's house at the junction of Woodstock Road, Cherryville Street, Jerry's Off-licence in Portallo Street, John Smith's fish and chip shop on the Albertbridge Road and Eddie Spence's fish and chip shop on the Beersbridge Road. On a wet Saturday night, tired and hungry after a long stand trying to keep the peace, when things quietened down, there was nothing better than to slip into the heat of the fish and chip kitchen through a back door and be presented with a lovely cod and chips in a newspaper and a cup of tea to wash it down. Needless to say, every care was taken to ensure that the shops were not broken into during the nightshift. Likewise, many happy hours were spent in Jerry's off licence, putting the world to rights over a bottle of stout outside the licencing hours as Jerry's guests, and it was a great place to meet and appreciate the feelings of many of the local people of influence. As a young constable, I picked up more from these places as to what was happening in the neighbourhood than I would have in a year on the beat. It was a tragedy that because of the sectarian situation which later developed, Jerry was forced to sell and leave the area. I have not met a more fair minded man who had not a bad word to say about anyone. The Imperial Cinema on the Cregagh Road was another place where the manager was delighted to see the local police attending and my wife and children couldn't believe how well they were treated on a night out.

In September, 1964, leading up to a general election, although I did not realise it at the time, there was a good example of the police being used for political purposes. The Republican Party had decided to fly a tricolour in the window of their headquarters on the Falls Road and the Rev. Ian Paisley threatened the Government that if it was not removed, he would march up the Falls Road with a crowd of his followers to remove it. The hardliners in the Government obviously agreed that the flag should be removed, notwithstanding it could only be seen if you were standing opposite the window. Republicans had gathered on the Falls Road to resist any attempt by Paisley and his followers and the police were subsequently ordered by the Government to remove the flag. This caused a great deal of resentment and there were numerous scuffles as the flag was taken down.

The republican youth on the Falls Road began to stone the

police and there were two nights of serious rioting when police from outside areas had to be drafted in. I remember being sent across to the Falls area in tenders, without adequate protection and being stoned incessantly by hundreds of young republicans with bricks, paving stones etc. All the police had was a baton, a twelve inch piece of wood, which was absolutely useless in the circumstances. Baton charges were organised but the youths disappeared into the side streets and reformed behind us again. Police were always heavily out-numbered at least ten to one and I resented the fact that reporters and news gatherer's cameras were generally pointing towards the police charging with batons and never towards the mobs who were stoning us. I remember about twenty of us running full tilt at a mob of about two hundred after heavy stoning. I was fast and well to the front when Sergeant McClelland grabbed me and told me to get back. He told me to watch the Head Constable who was Jack Hermon at the time and

Artists Impression Falls Road Riot

to follow him as he was the man in charge and not to be running in front. One of our party who had got separated from the rest was Constable Norman McQuade and he was badly beaten by the rioters who threatened to hang him. He was only rescued when landrovers from the reserve force scattered the lynch mob.

Police were continually running up and down the Falls Road getting nowhere near the rioters and were totally exhausted. I remember some of the residents who were sick of the rioting, actually shouting encouragement to the police. Unfortunately, police drafted in from other areas in their frustration, broke some residents' windows with their batons which did nothing to assist the local police who had to pick up the pieces in the aftermath. These events sowed the seeds for the beginning of the long terrorist campaign we were all to endure. Politically, the catholic vote was split and the unionist candidate was elected in West Belfast which appears to me to have been the result that Paisley had anticipated. He continued his ranting that the prime minister, Terence O'Neil must go because he met with Sean Lemass, and together with his anti Catholic rhetoric continued to keep the political pot at boiling point.

Sergeant McClelland had encouraged me to continue with my studies and was delighted when I eventually took first place at the Sergeants examination in 1965. 'Big Joe' had an intimate knowledge of the Willowfield area and while he worked hard, he also played hard. He used the 'F' word to excess, and was in fact barred from his Golf Club for three months for using it too much. Despite this, he had a heart of corn, was fond of his tipple and knew all the publicans, where he would often call after closing time. On one occasion on leaving a bar in the early hours, he arrested a fellow running past him with an armful of suits stolen from Gowdy's drapers shop on the Woodstock Road. The constable responsible for the beat who visited his lock-up shops religiously twice each night obviously had been watched and the break-in took place after he had passed.

After I qualified for Sergeant, John Creagmile introduced me to office work in the Sergeant's office to gain experience in dealing with paysheets, allocation of equipment, crime forms and all the other necessary tasks that would be required to act as a Sergeant. I was very grateful for this experience and for the next three years I assisted him and his typists, Elizabeth and Joan, in the office. At this time, the civil rights campaign was beginning to raise its head and there was a lot of civil unrest, particularly around the university. Looking back at that time, my feelings were that these people were breaking the law by obstructing the highways and should be dealt with by the law. There were no indications that this movement would be eventually taken over by subversives. The so called 'Peoples democracy' were demonstrating on issues such as 'one man one vote', unfair allocation of housing, gerrymandering county and district borders etc and bringing protesters on to the streets and blocking off main thoroughfares. I felt that there were lecturers at Queens University at that time with left wing tendencies who were influencing young fertile students' minds with revolutionary claptrap. While there were genuine grievances and attempts at peaceful protest, the act of bringing large numbers of students and young persons on the streets eventually got out of control and the civil rights movement was hi-jacked by those with more sinister motives, i.e. the overthrow of the state. This led to confrontation between protesters and police and the continuous anti-police propaganda witnessed over the past four decades, notwithstanding all of the so-called grievances such as one man one vote, gerry-mandering of boundaries etc, were dealt with within a very short period.

I began to play football again for the Castlereagh divisional team, 'F' Division, despite the plate in my leg. Inter-divisional matches were arranged and played on a monthly basis, as sports leave was available to anyone who was involved in sport. We had a reasonable team and enjoyed our monthly matches. I had also an interest in golf and had joined Mahee Island Golf Club. The

F. Division FC, 1964

police also had a golfing society of which I became a member, and as there was a monthly outing, my sporting activities of football and golf continued unabated. There was a notable increase of theft from cars in the 'F' Division area and on one occasion, Sergeant McClelland and I noticed a man acting suspiciously near cars at the flats where he lived. As we approached him he ran off and we separated to try and cut him off. However, he managed to give us the slip but when we got back to the station we looked through some photographs of likely suspects and recognised the man we were chasing as a known criminal from North Belfast. We informed the Detective Head Constable, John McCormick, who had the person brought in for interview. He admitted a number of crimes in the area and stolen property from other offences was recovered.

As a result of these detections, I was asked to help out the C.I.D. for a short period and worked with the local detectives, George Caskey, Bob Gunning and Wesley Cummings in Castlereagh. I gained some experience in detective work and particularly remember staking out a shop, suspected of receiving stolen goods in the form of cigarettes stolen from other properties. The methodology was the owner of the shop left the front door of the shop on the latch when closing his premises and the criminals broke into other premises, then left the stolen cigarettes in his shop on their way home. I did find out the door of the shop was left unsecured but on the occasions we had it under surveillance, we were either compromised or they called it off for some other reason.

After a time with C.I.D, I returned to office duties in the Sergeant's office in Willowfield and in 1968, was summonsed to a promotion board led by County Inspector Lanadale and included District Inspector Cordner and District Inspector Michael McAtamny. My name finally appeared on the list for promotion to Sergeant This was a bit of a surprise as my District Inspector, Tom Russell, although a decent man, continually started his report on promotion for me with the words, "The constable has comparatively short service" , then he went on to highlight all my good points but I always felt that his first sentence did me no favours, even though I had taken first place in the examination in 1965 and was by now mature at almost thirty years of age. It was not long before the names above me on the list moved on and I was next. At this stage, Marie and I waited with anticipation and excitement to see where I would be sent and finally, the note came through from Headquarters that I was promoted Sergeant and transferred to Springfield Road Station. I was delighted, firstly because I was remaining in Belfast, the experience I would get in a completely different area and the fact that we would not have to move house at this stage.

Chapter 6
(Springfield Road)

On the first of May, 1968, I travelled across Belfast, along the Grosvenor Road, across the Falls Road into the Springfield Road and turned left into Violet Street, about one hundred yards from the Falls/Springfield Road junction. I had been to R.U.C. central stores at Sprucefied and obtained my new uniform with the Sergeant's chevrons on my arm and I noticed the 'V' was upside down, something I had not noticed before. I felt a bit self conscious and apprehensive as the new young Sergeant and for good reason, as some of the most senior and street wise constables in the R.U.C were stationed there.

First impression of the station was that it was little more than a two storey house. It was about half way along Violet Street on the left and I was met at the door by the Station Sergeant, Paddy Rooney, a pleasant round faced, prematurely grey haired man who made me very welcome and it was not long before he put me at ease. He introduced me to Constable Johnny McNeill a mountain of a man, who had spent about forty years in the force, mostly at Springfield, and had also been a heavy weigh champion in the R.U.C. boxing team. The District Inspector in charge of the division was Frank Lagan, a good and decent officer who made me very welcome. I particularly remember when I was required to instruct about fifty divisional personnel, (take a school) on the new 1968 Road Traffic Act and was explaining my interpretation to the men, a high ranking officer who was sitting in at the school, contradicted my interpretation. Mr Lagan told him in no uncertain terms that he was wrong and the Sergeant was right. I thought this was a very brave thing to do on my behalf. The Head Constable in the area was Bob Gilchrist and I met two of the other Sergeants, Hutchinson and a man who was to become a very close friend, Sammy Leacock.

Springfield Road had a reputation of being a 'block' station, meaning that constables who had created problems at other Belfast Stations were generally sent to Springfield Road for their misdemeanours. I had personal experience of this while acting as Station Sergeant at a later date when it was decided to increase the staff at the station, and every station in Belfast took the opportunity to unload to Springfield Road those constables who they considered to be a problem. Nevertheless, I found that once they had settled in, and because of the nature of the area and the subsequent troubles, the camaraderie amongst the station party became excellent and they looked after one another. This applied throughout the police division which at that time also included Hastings Street, Andersonstown and Roden Street stations. My first job was that of a supervising Sergeant which consisted of looking after my own Section of about eight constables at Springfield. More often that not, because of annual leave and sickness etc, this number was depleted to about four constables for any one shift of duty. For the same reason, the supervising sergeant was often detailed to the district mobile patrol car, M2, which operated out of Hastings Street or M3, which operated out of Andersonstown. On these occasions, when no other Sergeant was available, which often happened on night duty, the responsibility for policing the whole division fell on the Sergeant in the patrol car. This included answering all '999'calls from Belfast Control Centre and dealing with all queries and calls from each station in the division. On many occasions, both cars worked together when back-up was required and I particularly remember the close liaison with Sergeant John Rowe who was in one car and I in the other.

There was some sectarian tension along the interface areas between Springfield Road and the Shankill Road and The Grosvenor Road and the Donegal Road but I was reasonably surprised that the local police in the area generally had a good rapport with the residents. Linfield football supporters, protestants, often walked from the Shankill Road across the catholic Falls Road area into

Grosvenor Road when they were playing Distillery and the only policing at that time was two Constables at each road junction. I had no difficulty in walking the beat on the Falls Road on my own or while doing supervision duties and made lots of useful contacts. At that time, bars closed at ten o'clock and on occasions, I went into premises such as the Bee-hive bar and the Celtic Bar on the Falls Road to remind them of the closing times and never had a problem with the patrons. In fact, the managers often requested it and were glad to use the police as an excuse to clear the pub and get home after a long day. The Constables also had their calling houses for tea and off- licences for an occasional tipple which was part of the reason for good relationships. The canteen at the Royal Victoria Hospital was often used and relations were maintained as the hospital staff liked to have the visible presence of police around the accident and emergency department, especially on evening and night duty. I am led to believe that on hot summer nights, nude bathing may have taken place in the swimming pool within the grounds of the hospital. I have still some very good friends in the area from relationships formed during my first years in Springfield Road.

Sergeant Bailie McGimpsey was stationed at Roden Street during this time and as he also played the piano keyed accordion, we became good friends. He introduced me to Johnny Morelli, who had an ice-cream shop on the Falls Road . Johnny, of Italian extraction, was an accordionist who loved nothing better than to have a session on the 'box' when I slipped in to his Falls Road shop for a cup of tea. Johnny had a Farfisa electronic accordion and was an excellent player who taught me some of the Italian classic accordion pieces. These are good memories although later events through sectarian unrest meant that it was dangerous for me to visit Johnny as often as I would have liked. When Johnny died during the height of the troubles, I made it my business to go to the wake in civilian clothes, which was much appreciated by the family, although they were quite concerned for my safety. I also made a point of walking after the coffin for a short distance at the funeral. Another popular musical place was the 'Wee House' bar in Albert Street where there was always traditional music going on and occasionally I would pull an overcoat over my uniform and call in to listen as I was a great lover of this type of music. At that time, you might have heard a rebel song followed by a protestant song and both would have been equally applauded.

I also recall on night duty, after midnight when things were quiet, driving along the Springfield Road and picking up a well known traditional violinist, Sean Maguire, after he had been performing

Entertaining at Springfield

at some show or other. He was introduced to me by Constable Errol Dunne who had taped many of his performances and it was amusing to see him with his violin stuck up his dark overcoat, creep out of the entry, looking right and left, then slipping into the back of the police car before anyone could see him. Sean had been in the old I.R.A but would not talk about his experiences. He loved to sit in the police station and play the violin with me on the accordion until the early hours and he was also a great story teller. Every tune he played had a story and there was also the occasional bottle of stout to quench our thirsts. Those were great times and he taught me a lot about traditional music and to play such reels as the 'Mason's Apron' and the 'Foxhunter.'

I found out about another accordionist who lived in Andersonstown and who played an electronic accordion called a Cordovox. I had heard this instrument on the radio and was impressed with the sound so one evening when things were quiet, I was supervising Sergeant in the police car with Constable John Moore driving and I decided to call at the house. The person I was looking for was not at home but his parents assured me he would not be long and invited me in to wait for him. They were a lovely family but we got a call from Control Room which meant we had to leave, but when we dealt with the call, we went back and the person I was looking for had arrived home. This was another surprisingly enjoyable occasion where we received so much hospitality and goodwill from the family and I was permitted to have a tune on the accordion. I was so impressed with the electronic accordion that I at once began to inquire as to where I might find one. I found there was one for sale in Millisle, owned by Benny Macauley, who ran a fun fair in the village. At the first opportunity, I headed down to Millisle with Marie and bought the Accordion.

A good friend to the Springfield Road police at that time was Jackie Vernon who had a butcher's shop at the corner of Springview Street and Springfield Road. Jackie had played centre half for West Bromwich Albion and for Northern Ireland for many years and was a great character on the Springfield Road. I had the pleasure of watching him play for the Great Britain team against the Rest of the World team at Windsor Park. There were many enjoyable evenings spent in Beacom's bar at the corner of Falls Road and Springfield Road listening to himself and Charlie Tully the Celtic and Northern Ireland wing forward, recalling incidents from their old footballing days. On early shifts at break time, the first call in the morning was to go across to Jackie's for a pound of sausages and a pound of bacon for a good fry. I can still smell the aroma of those sausages and bacon floating across Violet Street. Unfortunately, the situation later arose that Jackie was warned off by evil men that it would not be a good idea to have police going into his premises to buy food and for his sake police stopped going into his butcher's shop.

I was still interested in promotion and after serving a year as a Sergeant, I was permitted to sit the examination for Head Constable. This I did in April, 1969, and was lucky enough to take third place. At that time, the pass mark required was seventy per-cent in each of the three papers so I was delighted to qualify at the examination although a bit disappointed when a number of Sergeants with fifteen years service who had not taken the exam were promoted that year before those who qualified. On reflection, they were worthy of their promotions because of their service but it annoyed me that Tommy Gracey, a Sergeant who also passed the examination and had more than fifteen years service, was overlooked in favour of someone who did not take the examination. However, this was the last year that long service, (fifteen years) was a factor in promotion so these men deserved to be considered and I was delighted that Sammy Leacock my good friend and colleague was promoted Head Constable on long service as I considered him to be an excellent ambassador for the police service.

Policing in 'B' Division was beginning to become exceedingly difficult. The civil rights campaign was continuing to gather momentum and while there were genuine grievances held by many, there were also signs that subversives were infiltrating the movement. Gangs of young protestants began to gather on the Protestant side of Cupar Street which in turn led to similar gangs on the Catholic side and police duties in the evening period was generally taken up by trying to keep them apart. This progressed from cat-calling to stone throwing and police manpower was stretched. Political ranting still went on and in fact did the police no favours, neither did the religious leaders in either community. On one particular 11th July, night, I paraded the men and had appointed two to the Cupar Street area. I knew there was a Head Constable from Tennent Street who would be supervising and I told the men to be sure to stay on the beat until he had seen them and moved on. Generally, when things quietened down in the early hours, it was possible to call into their calling houses and have a quiet drink but I emphasised that they on no account were to leave their beat until the Head had passed.

On this specific night, things were particularly quiet and the Head sure enough arrived and went out with me to inspect the men on the beat. However we walked up and down Cupar Street three times and no men were to be seen. As we passed Lynagh's off-licence for the fourth time the door began to be furtively opened and the Head stuck his stick in the door thus stopping it from being closed. In we went and there were the two constables standing at the bar. I persuaded him that I would discipline them both in my own way and he left it to me to deal with. He in fact was anxious to get back to his own area where he had probably a drink arranged for later and if these two idiots had done what they were told, he would have been long gone.

On another evening, a group of thugs from the protestant side came across to the Falls Road and caused a lot of damage by smashing shop windows before heading back along Northumberland Street to their own area. I was supervising Sergeant in the district mobile car with Constable John Moore as driver and Constable Fred Mahood as extra observer. We received the call and went to the scene. A large crowd had gathered on the Falls Road and Jim Sullivan, a known official I.R.A. republican was acting as spokesman. He intimated the perpetrators had just gone into the protestant area so we followed along and found five or six youths walking along the street. We stopped them and were questioning them about their movements and believed we had grounds to arrest for disorderly behaviour, when a large number of residents came out and began to lay into us. The weight of numbers forced us to withdraw from the area and when we went back to the Falls Road crowd empty handed, they began also to take their frustrations out on us. We pointed out to Sullivan that we had been beaten up in the protestant area and prisoners taken from us by the crowd which he could clearly see from the state of our uniforms. I assured him that if he would assist to disperse the Catholic crowd, the identity of the perpetrators were known to me and they would be arrested at a later date. He addressed the catholic crowd in Irish and they dispersed peacefully.

The following day, Fred Mahood and I went to the Cumberland Inn in Northumberland Street and lo and behold, there was one of the youths who had been involved the previous evening. We brought him to Hastings street station where he was charged with disorderly behaviour and lodged in the police office. The following morning he appeared at Belfast Custody Court and was convicted of disorderly behaviour. This action resulted in quietening a very volatile situation for the time being but such incidents began to occur on a nightly basis and it became exceedingly difficult for police to keep tabs on everything that was happening.

I was still travelling across town from Cregagh at this time and I began to consider moving to somewhere more convenient. Marie and I looked at houses in Mizen Gardens in the Lenadoon Estate in Andersonstown and we decided to move to number sixteen. There were a number of policemen living convenient to the area so we felt that it was a good move. My elder daughters Valerie and

Gwen, were in the process of moving to Carolan Grammar School as they had both qualified at the eleven plus exams so we arranged for Carol to change from Cregagh to Suffolk Primary School. Marie made friends quickly with neighbours and we attended Suffolk Presbyterian Church. Unfortunately, Carol's education suffered as it appeared Cregagh School was so far ahead of Suffolk that she had practically nothing to do the first year and I believe was not extended to her potential. The house was an excellent house, much better layout than the previous one and we were very happy there for a time. Constable Stanley Corry lived in Horn Walk, just around the corner and Constable Matt Ward, another friend lived in a bungalow not far from us. Stanley and I in our leisure time often played golf at Dunmurry nine hole golf course together with Tommy Fleming and Adrian Ringland. Walter Bruce was the professional at the club and there were concession fees for police.

Travelling to work now was much easier along the Falls Road to Springfield Road. However, leisure time became less and less as the sectarian rantings from either side increased and police were more often than not required for duty each evening. There was no overtime at this time nor were there any provisions to feed us. Instructions for parades and such were usually accompanied by the phrase, "Haversack rations will be carried:" meaning that you were expected to fend for yourself. Interface tensions increased on a nightly basis with Cupar Street the battle area, between the Shankill and Springfield Roads. Patrols were increased through using men on twelve hour shifts and sometimes working up to sixteen hours. This was the long hot summer that the civil rights agitators had promised and unfortunately, the weather, which often comes to the assistance of the police, was indeed warm and sunny throughout the whole summer. Rioting became a constant occurrence and police manpower was at full stretch.

Following the infamous civil rights march to Londonderry, rioting took place in the town. All available police were rounded up and sent to Londonderry on 12th August, 1969. District Inspector

Frank Lagan, was in charge of the contingent from "B" division and he asked me to stay close to him. When we arrived there was serious rioting taking place in the Bogside and the Reserve force was taking the brunt of extremely hostile attacks on the police. We were deployed at Butcher's Gate and our instructions were to secure that entrance, keep the rioters in the bog-side and not allow the rioting to spill out into the town. I distinctly remember seeing the leading civil rights female at the time, amongst a crowd breaking concrete paving stones on the roof of the flats and hurling them at the unfortunate police below. We were on this point for a period of thirty six hours or more, and most were totally exhausted, even though the brunt of the attacks on police was lower down in the bog-side. The rioters were better organised than us as they worked in shifts and shouted they would see us in the morning when they left to go to bed. We were left to lie on our shields during lulls in the rioting. There were hundreds of rioters and there were about two dozen of us at Butcher's Gate. We could not have repelled any sustained attack, lucky for us, only sporadic attacks occurred throughout the night and we managed to keep the rioters in their own area.

After forty eight hours of continuous duty in Londonderry without relief, rioting had broken out in Belfast and we were sent home in tenders. I got home to Mizen Gardens on 14th August, 1969 and fell into bed exhausted. I had been fifty seven hours on continuous duty and apparently I slept for about fifteen hours and Marie refused to wake me. When I awoke, I immediately got back into uniform and headed off for Springfield Road. I was unaware that all hell had broken loose in Belfast on the night of the 14thinst when a large crowd of protestants who had assembled in Dover street were fired on by a number of men from St Comgall's primary school on the Falls Road and one of them, Herbie Roy, whom I had known as a hard line loyalist when he resided at the bottom of the Woodstock Road, was fatally injured. Consequently, police who were of the opinion that the I.R.A. was mounting a serious attack on the state, replied to this attack by deploying shoreland jeeps with heavy machine guns mounted and fired on the school.

Later, in the early hours of 15th August, constables who were on the roof of Hastings Street Station, reported by radio that they were being fired on from the roof of Divis Flats. On the second occasion they returned fire and a British soldier, trooper Hugh McCabe who was home on leave, was fatally injured. A young boy living in Divis Flats, Patrick Rooney, was also tragically killed by a stray bullet as a result of all this fire power. Subsequent statements to the Scarman Tribunal suggested that Hugh McCabe with others had been throwing missiles at police on the street below but the tribunal concluded that gunfire had also come from the roof of the flats and that the firing that killed Mr McCabe was justified.

I was unaware of these events as I drove along the Falls Road citywards towards Springfield Road Station to report for duty the evening of 15th August. Burnt out cars were forming barricades at every road junction and when I reached the Falls/Springfield junction, there was a large crowd of about one hundred rioters hijacking buses and cars. I removed my revolver from its holster and put it on the seat beside me to be handy. I drove at the crowd which scattered although many tried to stop me and managed to turn the corner left into Springfield Road, then again left into Violet Street where there was an army type vehicle parked, keeping the road open. I managed to get into the Station in Violet Street, little did I know I would be there for two weeks. Things got so bad in the area that I rang my wife Marie and told her to take the children to her mother's house in Comber until I contacted her again. There were three constables in the station and the Station Sergeant Paddy Rooney and his wife. Paddy at this time had been promoted to Head Constable and he was in charge of a moth ball (armoured car) in Hastings Street, so I was left in charge of the station. My instructions were to remain in the station with the three men and protect the station. A complaint was received from a woman of rioting in Bombay Street and I contacted Control at Belfast and asked them to send a vehicle to the area. I was told they would respond and told the woman that police were on their way.

Eventually, a patrol arrived at Bombay Street but the damage and evacuation had already commenced. Houses had been set on fire by maurauding protestants who had dispersed by the time the police arrived and the police were told to 'Fuck off'. There was little the completely undermanned police could do at that stage. Half the force of two thousand had been injured and the army had already been called into Londonderry and were about to be called into Belfast. I distinctly remember on the evening of 15th August, standing out at the junction of Violet Street / Springfield Road and watching the first army regiment marching down the Springfield Road in full battledress, taking up the whole of the Road, an impressive sight, and the catholic crowds cheering on each side of the road as they marched past. I greeted the Captain at the door of Springfield Road Station. The new station had just been built and the army occupied it. At that time, I was convinced that the troubles would be over in a year. How wrong was I?

Initially there were reasonable relationships between the police and army but then it became apparent to police that we were being treated as under suspicion. In one of my conversations with one of the army officers he informed me that his instructions were to beware of a revolutionary police force. This was unbelievable as I could not see any member of the Royal Ulster Constabulary being a revolutionary. Admittedly, there were a few members who had hard line protestant tendencies, but these had been stoked by the continuous aggression towards police from republicans from the mainly catholic side of the community. The evidence of these assumptions on the part of the army were constantly borne out by events throughout the first two years. I was stopped going home to my house in Mizen Gardens in Andersonstown, by a military patrol. I was in police uniform and asked if I was armed. I stated I was and the corporal asked me to give up my weapon. I refused, stating I needed my weapon for my own and my family's protection. He then went to the crowd of youths who were loitering at the corner of the Donegal Road/Springfield Road and asked them if I could proceed. I saw them shaking their heads in a negative fashion and he again came to me and asked me to give up my weapon. I refused and asked to speak to his superior officer. A Lieutenant arrived and I was eventually allowed to proceed. This is one of many situations that occurred at that time and it was clear to me that the British Government and the army were completely misled by the anti police propaganda and biased reporting of events.

On another occasion, a military patrol was maliciously informed that a terrorist lived in a particular house on the front of the Stewartstown Road which in fact was occupied by a policeman, Constable Alex Young. An army patrol broke down the front door and Alex, thinking it was an I.R.A attack confronted them with his weapon at the top of the stairs. Only some quick thinking and restraint by both parties prevented what would have ended in fatalities. These are examples of many incidents where military listened to and acted on malicious rumour and gossip from those with ulterior motives.

Notwithstanding, it was still important to continue to endeavour to police but it was difficult when army was so ill informed. This suited those that were intent in overthrowing the state. The police still had contacts within the community and I as Station Sergeant was invited to perform by playing the accordion at a concert in St Paul,s hall, Cavendish Street, by the local priest, Father Murray. This I did in uniform and army officers also attended. The three girls on before me were from the bog-side in Derry and they got a tremendous reception so I was a bit apprehensive. However, when my turn came to perform, I was given a great reception and really enjoyed the night. However, in the passing of time, those contacts were put under pressure and all but lost and the radicals lost no time in turning the locals against the army. Through now intense anti-british propaganda, the army moved from being the saviours of the catholic people to the British Bastards who were stamping the British jackboot on the poor catholic people of the Falls Road. Unfortunately, certain members of the catholic church who were born on the Falls Road and who could have helped to curtail the rioting and civil unrest, believed the ideals of the then forming provisional I.R.A. were in the best interests of the church and were suspicious of the 'communist and social tendencies' of the official I.R.A. I do believe had a particular Cardinal made a concerted attempt to stop the unrest, together with any protestant clergy willing to commit themselves to good relationships with their catholic neighbours, we may not have had the thirty years of bloodshed we have since experienced.

Springfield Road police station became the centre for new army regiments every four months while the police continuously bore the brunt of the catholic hostility because of constant and expert provisional I.R.A. propaganda. Unfortunately most of the army officers in charge saw the four month tour as an opportunity to make their names in this turbulent situation. Many of the decisions made by the military were queer to say the least and most were made with little or no police input. Notwithstanding, it was important to continue as normal as possible and everyday policing chores still had to be dealt with. Some time after Paddy Rooney's promotion to Head, Sergeant Hutchison was moved to Roden Street and I was appointed Station Sergeant. My assistants were Helen Baird, chief clerk, and Liz Shilliday, assistant clerk. The routine duties included reading the occurrence book every morning, deciding which entry amounted to a crime and entering a Form 38, which was forwarded to C.I.D. Entries which required further uniformed police action would then be assessed and appropriate action decided and those entries which required no further action would be written off. Each person at the station had a store card which recorded all the public property that has been issued to them such as weapons, tunics, shirts ties and all sorts of equipment. Every so often, personnel were entitled to replacement uniforms, shirts etc., and a record was kept of each date they became due and each person was subsequently sent to Sprucefield Central Store to have everything updated.

There were never enough hours in the day to get through everything that a Station Sergeant had responsibility for. The duty sheet for every person in the Station was made out a month in advance which took into consideration sickness, requests for annual leave etc., but the main headache was the preparation of the pay sheets which included basic pay, overtime, deductions of National Insurance, graduated pension scheme, pension contributions, income tax and all other miscellaneous deductions which were calculated in respect of each person. Different rates of wages depended on rank and service and each person's details were hand written on a large sheet of paper with appropriate headings. Each month, the preparation of the pay sheets began about the middle of the month and when all the deductions had been made it was then that the amount needed of each denomination of pounds, shillings and pence were calculated in total. On the last day of the month, pay day, I went to the bank with my little black bag and handed the teller a list containing the number of twenty pound notes, ten pound notes, various change etc., that was required and on return to the station, the door of the office was locked until all the pay envelopes were filled and sealed and there were no shortages or left-overs. Only then was the door opened and the constables collected their pay. I would calculate there must be at least thirty people in the civil service now doing what the Station Sergeant and his two clerks did at that time. When overtime started to be paid, I remember the first red hundred pound notes being issued.

Policing remained extremely difficult and everyone from the top down was under pressure because of the inability to do their job properly. It was important to arrange activities to relieve the pressure and Divisional Football was one of those activities. Contact was made with the then Merseyside constabulary to arrange a match with their officers and they were delighted to host a week-end away for the 'B' Division football team. Brian Dunlop and Hilton Foote organised the team and we travelled to Merseyside, [now Liverpool & Bootle] and were met by Geoff Swinerton and George Johnston who had organised the trip on their side. We were royally treated and what started as a one-off trip, became an annual event. The Liverpool police had great empathy with our predicament and went out of their way to give us a really good time. It was during one of these matches that I was subject to a blocked tackle when kicking the ball and I felt a shudder go up my left leg which had previously been broken with the plate inserted. I decided at this point that my football days were over and I began to concentrate on golf as an alternative. I was still a member of the R.U.C. Golfing Society and Mahee Island Golf Club and was able to avail of a days Sports leave per month to play in the police outings.

Major changes were taking place in the R.U.C. and in October, 1969, following the Hunt report which disarmed the police and

'B Division F.C. 1970

disbanded the Ulster Special Constabulary, the rank structure was changed. The numbers were to be doubled, the rank of Inspector General changed to Chief Constable and County Inspector to Assistant Chief Constable. The rank of District Inspector became Superintendent, Head Constable changed to Chief Inspector and Inspector. I was disappointed at this because I had qualified at the Head Constable's exam which required seventy per-cent of a pass mark and this was reduced to forty per-cent to the rank of Inspector to bring it into line with English forces. The disbanding of the 'B' Special Constabulary had repercussion in that rioting took place in the protestant Shankill Road and when the police endeavoured to contain those riots, constable Victor Arbuckle was shot dead by so called loyalists.

Sir Arthur Young had been appointed as Chief Constable by the British Government and adopted a policy of 'Softly Softly', which in fact meant he had agreed with the local official I.R.A. that there would be no police in catholic areas. I recall answering a call with John Moore in the police vehicle to Leeson Street when shots had been fired and we came across a green car which we recognised as belonging to a well-known provisional with the radiator still warm. It had no doubt been involved in the shooting but we were accosted by William Sullivan, the brother of Jim Sullivan, a well known official I.R.A man who stated that they had a meeting with Sir Arthur Young who had agreed that no police should go into that area. This was obviously a dispute between the Officials and Provos but again we were helpless to do anything. I eventually interviewed that owner of the car but without the ability to make inquiries and obtain evidence in the area, nothing could be proved.

When Sir Arthur Young left in 1970, (I considered him to be a political appointment to see in the disarming of the R.U.C,) the new Chief Constable appointed was Graham Shillington. On one occasion, when there was rioting at the rear of Hastings Street Station, it transpired that only myself and John Moore were left in the station. The station came under attack from a riotous mob and we broke into the arms room and managed to get a Sterling gun and I stood inside the front door. John got on the telephone to police control to ask for assistance. By this time, I could see the door was on fire by the rim of fire around the perimeter and someone was trying to break the door down with a hatchet as it was protruding through the door with each blow. I became aware of someone over my right shoulder and on looking around, I saw the then Commissioner, Mr Shillington, later to become Chief Constable, standing with his pistol drawn behind me, obviously nervous and pointing it at the door. I don't know where he came from but I could see I was not going to get any directions so I turned to him and said, "Sir, if that door comes in, I intend to open fire".. He made no reply but luckily a reserve force patrol arrived from the city centre and dispersed the mob before they gained entry.

As I.R.A. activity, bombings and attacks on the police continued, there was a lot of disquiet about the disarming of the police in the area who now felt they were left without adequate protection. There were impromptu meetings held at Hastings Street and I remember one meeting addressed by a Sergeant from the Drugs Squad who was adamant that police should demand that they be given their weapons back to defend themselves. The police were to be re-armed eventually, but the bombing and shootings continued unabated. Throughout 1970, there were numerous incidents of terrorism. A man alleged to have been throwing petrol bombs was shot by the army in a riot near Balaclava Street and attacks on police and army became nightly occurrences.

Brown Square Police station was bombed in January and in July, the army imposed a curfew in the lower Falls area in Belfast and began a search for weapons. As station sergeant at this time, I found this to be a problem in that the army lifted all weapons, many of which were legally held with firearms certificates, and deposited them in different places in the station. I had many decent people who were in no way connected with terrorism, coming to me and complaining that their 'Churchill' shotguns, some worth a lot of money, had been seized by the army and they had no idea where they were. I managed to sort most of them out but this action caused a lot of resentment in the ordinary population which we could have well done without and in fact recruited more young radicals to the provisional I.R.A.

The deaths of Constables Samuel Donaldson and Robert Millar at Crossmaglen on 12th August, 1970 caused great anxiety throughout the force. These two constables were well respected in the area, and their deaths met with mixed reactions from the people of Crossmaglen. It is important to acknowledge that there were many floral wreaths sent by local people to the homes of the murdered constables. On 25th May, 1971, a man in his mid twenties threw a blast bomb into the reception area at Springfield road Police Station. Inspector Ted Nurse was there and he immediately tried to get a woman and two children in the foyer away from the scene by directing them down the corridor towards the rear of the station past the area where Sergeant Willets was sitting at a desk in the corridor. The bomb exploded and a locker convenient to Sergeant Willets sitting in the corridor caused his death. I was in the Sergeant's office at the time which was at the end of the corridor a short distance from the tragedy. There was a great feeling of apprehension in the minds of all police in the area in that attacks were being made not only on police on duty but their homes and relatives were also being targeted.

It was not long before I had the misfortune to loose the first very close friend at Springfield Road. Stanley Corry had been a friend since I moved to the station. He lived in Doon Road, just around the corner from my house at Mizen Gardens and was my golfing partner. On the 1st November, 1971, Stanley put his head round the door of my office in Springfield Road and said he had got a call to a break- in at a boutique in Andersonstown but there were no other detectives to go with him and he needed someone as back-up. I told him I would go with him but I was finishing some paper work which would take ten minutes. He said he would wait but in about five minutes, he put his head round the door again and said that Eddie Russell had come in and would go with him. In less than fifteen minutes, I was informed they had both been shot dead in Andersonstown as it was a bogus call. Twenty-one spent cartridges were found at the scene. This was a stark eye-opener as to what faced each police officer in this area at the time. I was put in charge of the funeral arrangements for Stanley and the funeral party by the then Assistant Chief Constable Jimmy Flanagan. It was an extremely sad occasion and as his coffin was lowered, I took possession of the union flag that draped it. I still have the flag to this day. Stanley was buried with full police honours and many police and civilians lined the route. It was shortly after this that the decision was taken to re-arm the police for their own protection, which I must say was not what the majority of police wanted, but the situation demanded it.

Around this time, Paddy Devlin, the local representative, rang me at about 4.45pm one Friday evening and asked me to provide a police escort for him as he was going to appear on a UTV programme which might be controversial. I asked him what time he was appearing and he said in about thirty minutes. I told him it was impossible to arrange an escort in that time but that I and another constable would come along and look after him. I got the hold of Albert Burns and drove to UTV Studio. Paddy was already inside and he explained what he had to say on Television might provoke a reaction from local residents when he was leaving. I arranged for his car to be taken to the Ormeau Embankment by Albert and I told him I would pick him up in my car outside the door when the broadcast was finished and then change over on the Ormeau Embankment. He thought this was fine and brought me into a Mr Finnegan's office where politicians from all the different parties were assembled. They were all on first name terms and were laughing and joking in a very friendly manner. They were called into the television studio and as I watched on a monitor,

I could'nt believe how their attitude changed as they harangued each other.

When the interview was over, they returned to Finnegan's office and resumed their socializing as before. I remember thinking at the time that the general public on each side of the religious divide were being hoodwinked in the interest of getting votes. I got my car and drove to the front door and Paddy ran out and got into the passenger seat. There were only about four or five women who had gathered to shout abuse at him. We drove off and I dropped him at his own car in Ormeau Embankment and he thanked us and drove off. The following Monday morning, I got a call from Commissioner's office that Paddy had reported being fired on after he left us. I rang Gerry Fitt and asked him did he know anything about this. He told me Paddy had been asked to appear at a Provisional's meeting at Casement Park over the week-end and didn't want to do it so he possibly made this up as an excuse and cleared off to Donegal for the week-end. I still don't know the truth of the matter.

Chapter 7
(Community Relations)

On 1.12.71 I was promoted to the rank of Inspector and joined the Community Relations Branch at the Station. My basic pay went from£159.50 to £177.00 per month, a huge rise of £17.50. Leo McBrien and John (Bap) Dunlop had already been working at Community Relations and been endeavouring to keep contact with various organisations in the West Belfast area. John Dunlop was particularly well-known and respected as he played football for Glentoran and had a cheery word for all people he met in the area. However, it was in the interests of subversives to cut contact between police and the public so it was an ever ending struggle to make any headway with the population, two or three steps forward, then threats to those who were showing signs of getting to grips with the problem and we had to take three or four steps back. There were many decent people who were interested in keeping contact but the threat of death from the provisional I.R.A was too much for most to contemplate.

Leo McBrien was in the act of leaving his wife off at the Royal Victoria Hospital when a gunman fired a revolver through the driver's window of his car hitting him in the cheekbone. He managed to drive to Springfield Station and collapsed in the yard. He was taken immediately to the Royal Victoria Hospital where he was operated on and the bullet lodged in his cheekbone was taken out through the roof of his mouth. He was so lucky to have escaped with his life. These were the circumstances each of the police officers in Springfield, Roden Street, Andersonstown and Hastings Street had to face when going to or coming from the station or when out trying to do their duty. Every call had to be treated as a lure or 'come on' until it was proved otherwise.

Brian Lally, whose father Charlie had been a policeman on the Falls Road, eventually joined the Community Relations Branch on promotion to Sergeant when John Dunlop left and for the next two years, we endeavoured to maintain contact with groups in the area who were interested in law and order. People in the area were still being arrested for questioning in relation to terrorist offences and it was important to set up some sort of liaison for those who were worried about relations and friends. The C.R. branch became the go between for those inquiries and dealt with numerous inquiries. There were allegations of ill-treatment at Holywood barracks and R.U.C. Special Branch bore the brunt of these allegations. My own knowledge of Special Branch interrogators in the past was that the ill-treatment of prisoners would amount to a clip around the ear or a 'dig in the bake'. Such treatments as standing for long periods with a bag over your head, or being subjected to loud piercing noises for a prolonged period was not within the scope of police in Northern Ireland and would suggest to me that if this did happen, it was introduced by the military who had been given control. I knew a lot of the members of Special Branch at that time and would be surprised if they were in any way responsible for or condone such behaviour. I do not wish to portray the impression that all special branch members were angels, in every walk of life there are a few black sheep but then, police are recruited from civilians, and not all civilians walk the straight and narrow. However, my experience was that the miscreants in the police at that time were the exception rather than the rule.

There were few arrests for terrorist activities because of the fear in the population to give evidence and a decision was made probably in England that detectives from the Metropolitan Police should be drafted in to show the R.U.C. how it should be done. A superintendent and other non-commissioned officers arrived and in a few weeks, three leading provisionals were arrested, supposedly found in possession of a weapon. These men were convicted and one of the detectives when questioned as to what the accused had said after arrest was purported to have said, "fair cop guv"; It is hard to believe that a Falls Road man would come out with this obviously cockney expression. I was always dubious about why these officers were imported from the Met although I had no close contact with them but was not surprised when the senior officer in charge was later jailed for corruption on his return to the Metropolitan Police.

Because of the attacks on homes of serving members, in December, 1971 special extra plain clothes patrols were organised in each area during evenings and nights. This was an extra burden on police who were now also required to look after the area in which they lived. It was in addition to their normal duty so was an additional duty which they could have done without. Many inquiries from Paddy Devlin and Gerry Fitt in relation to arrests in the area were dealt with in the first couple of months in 1972 and an attempt to bomb the station was again made on the evening of 7th February with no injuries. I went back to the Station to survey the damage and the next day was spent dealing with requests from residents in Violet Street to have their property boarded up and secured.

There were many meetings with members of Community Groups regarding requests for C.R. funds and assistance to set up youth clubs in the Riverdale and Ballymurphy areas. At that time, P.I.R.A .members Jim Bryson and Tommy Tolan were armed and used by the provisionals to fire on the army and police from the Ballymurphy area and because of their ruthlessness, were successful in holding most of the residents to ransom. It took brave people to be seen negotiating with the police or other Government Departments. Bryson and Tolan were well known as criminals and bullies to the Andersonstown police long before the troubles began. These gangsters were given status by the provisional I.R.A and often drove around the estate toting armalite rifles and were responsible for army and police deaths. There was information that Bryson had been responsible for firing on Constable Abraham whom as Station Sergeant I had directed to New Barnsley Station as a recruit and luckily the bullet was deflected downwards by the heavy duty wire fence around the station and struck the constable in the leg. Eventually Bryson and another person, Patrick Mulvenna, were killed in a gun battle with the army in 1973 and there is still speculation that they were becoming too big for their boots and were set up by the Official I.R.A. Tolan was eventually shot dead in a feud in 1977 between the Officials and Provisionals.

By this time, Sir Jamie Flanagan (a catholic) had taken over as Chief Constable from Mr Shillington. He was a very popular officer within the force, involved with all the sporting organisations and I was involved in an incident which made me realise how approachable he really was. At the time, I was trying to bring people from the catholic Twinbrook and protestant East Belfast communities together. A lady from one of the catholic organisations mentioned to me that she and a delegation would like to meet the Chief Constable. I thought this would be a good opportunity for the Chief to get across his message as to what we were trying to achieve so I told her I would try to arrange it. I spoke to the Chief Constable's office and word came back that he would be delighted to meet the delegation. Arrangements were made and I took the delegation to Headquarters at Knock on the duly appointed date. Sir Jamie treated the women to tea and biscuits and could not have been more charming. In fact, he had them eating out of his hand and the ladies went back to the Twinbrook area with a completely different perspective as to what we were trying to achieve. I had the pleasure of playing golf with Sir Jamie long after he retired and he still recalled that particular meeting.

Incidents of bombings, shootings and sectarian murders were a weekly occurrence and in this atmosphere, each of the Community Relations branch members in the area was under a lot of stress. There was no counselling or other activities for relief so when incidents occurred, they were dealt with to the best of our ability and afterwards, the army mess was generally visited and a bottle of spirits obtained and shared as a way of winding down. Following one bombing on the station, I was entering the yard from the back door when a bomb was thrown into the yard and exploded. I looked up and my first thoughts were why was the glass in the upstairs windows bulging outwards and breaking, rather that breaking inwards. Fortunately, there were no casualties on that occasion and four of us, three senior officers and I retired to the community relations office and the boss sent to the army mess for a bottle of whisky. When I offered to pay my share I was politely told that I could buy a bottle in my turn. This was the means used to deal with the stress at that time.

We continued to try to make new contacts and keep those we already had. The provisional I.R.A. stepped up their hate campaign against the police whom they saw as a danger to their objectives and made life very difficult for those local people who were endeavouring to improve conditions in the area. It suited P.I.R.A propaganda to keep the population under poor conditions and under their control. Police houses in the Lenadoon area came under attack so I was forced into moving my family to a safer area. I decided to move to Kerrymount Avenue, off the Saintfield Road and managed to get together a deposit from the Ulster Bank and buy a house at number twenty. This made travelling across town to work much more difficult but it was worth the extra hassle to know that my family were safer. My son, Gary Thomas, was born here on 4th July, 1972 and we were all delighted to have a boy after three girls. By this time, Carol my youngest girl was twelve years old and both Valerie and Gwendoline were continuing with their education at Carolan Grammar School on the Ormeau Road.

During the last couple of months in 1972 I was asked to go to police headquarters to assist with office duties. This was handy for travelling purposes but while I was there, another good friend, Robert Nicholl, a detective constable at Springfield Road, was shot dead in tragic circumstances. He was driving along Castle Street and at the junction of Queen Street, he failed to see a military patrol signalling him to stop and he was fatally injured. This brought back to me the circumstances in which my grandfather had been shot. Robert's father, Willie was a Sergeant who had worked with me at Willowfield so I attended the house to offer my condolences and also went to Robert's funeral. When I returned to Springfield Road, it had been decided that a community relations presence was necessary in the Dunmurry police area which included the protestant Seymour Hill and the catholic Riverdale and Twinbrook areas.

I was transferred to Dunmurry on 19th February, 1973 and began to try and build up contacts and relationships. Superintendent John Barr and Chief Inspector Sam McFarland were in charge and I met some of the local clergy and lay people who were involved in Community Projects. Professor Muskett, Mr Bob Common, the Reverend Houston McKelvey and Sadie Patterson of Women Together, were all involved in trying to foster good relations and I had many discussions which proved most helpful. I was also involved with pensioners and youth clubs in each area and where Government money was available, organised joint ventures between clubs of the different religions. Suffolk and Taughmonagh were two protestant areas where the local protestant population felt under threat. We were often involved in meetings with the Community Associations in each of these areas and were under no illusions that they were possibly the front for organisations such as the U.D.A and/or U.V.F. Nevertheless, it was important to try and improve the living conditions in each of these areas and when we were speaking to the chairman of a community association, it was not difficult to work out that the paramilitaries were not far away, behind the scenes, running the show. The same applied in the Catholic areas such as Riverdale and Twinbrook with the Officials and Provisionals.

Bt this time, I had managed to purchase an 'A' Line seven berth caravan from Tom Turkington who owned Sandycove caravan site between Millisle and Ballywalter. The van was situated one back from the waters edge on the extreme right hand side of the site. Marie and the children went to the caravan for the two months of the school holidays and many happy days

were spent there. Unfortunately, pressure of work meant that I could not be there as often as I would have wished, but the children had a great time and made many friends. I also managed to purchase a small boat and whatever leisure hours we could squeeze in resulted in fishing and swimming and rowing round to Ballywalter. We really enjoyed our summers in Sandycove which gave some respite from the rigours and pressures at work.

Bombings and shootings continued throughout 1973 and on 10th May, 1974, two colleagues of mine, constables Malcolm Ross and Brian Bell from Dunmurry Station were on patrol at Finaghy crossroads. A hi-jacked car containing a number of armed terrorists drew up close to them and got out of the car and fired on the two constables. Both fell to the ground and an eye witness confirmed that when one of the terrorists saw a constable move, he walked over to him and shot him in the head at point blank range. The gunmen then drove off along Finaghy Road North where the car was later found abandoned. Two men, Vincent Hetherington and Myles McGrogan were later charged with the murders but escaped conviction on a technicality. However, both men were later killed by the I.R.A. as suspected informers to security forces. I was involved in the early stages of the investigation into the murders of Constables Bell and Ross through contacts in the Riverdale and Andersonstown areas but there was very little forthcoming from an evidential point of view as any body with any knowledge were too frightened to come forward and give evidence due to the fear factor and the stranglehold the provisional I.R.A. had on the community.

The following week, the U.V.F planted car bombs in both Dublin and Monaghan with devastating results. Thirty three people were killed as a result of these car bomb attacks and reverberations went round the world. The planning and implementation of these attacks were such that gave rise to suspicions that the loyalist organisations were incapable of such a well planned and successful terrorist operation and that there may have been some Army or security forces input. This suggestion was later given some credence when two army officers from the press and security services alleged that British Security services had assisted in the attacks. However, this was denied by both the British and Irish governments, although relatives of the dead and injured did not appear to accept the official line and continue to try and find evidence to the contrary.

There were still a lot of killings during the remainder of 1974 and a lot of pressure in dealing with both sides of the community and trying to bring them closer together. I was not aware of being under stress at the time as we just continued to work night and day but in retrospect, I was probably burning the candle at both ends so to speak. One evening, Marie had gone out and I was lying on the couch, chain smoking as usual, (I had been getting through eighty cigarettes a day) and watching television. I went to get up from the couch and I was suddenly hit in the middle of the chest by the most enormous pain which knocked me down on to my knees. I knew immediately I had a heart attack but I could do nothing about it. I remained on the floor until I heard Marie at the door and then tried to make it onto a chair before she came in. I asked her to go across the road and get the doctor who lived there as I suspected I was having a heart attack. Marie saw my condition and ran out immediately. The doctor was not available so I told her to take me to the Ulster Hospital and she drove me there. I managed to walk in through the door but was ushered into a wheel chair and taken to emergency where it was confirmed that I had indeed had a coronary. When the doctor heard the amount of cigarettes I smoked he told me that if I hadn't smoked, I would not have had the attack. I decided at that moment that I would not smoke again. I remained in the hospital for about ten days then went home to recuperate. In all, I was off work for about a month and a half and the Chief Superintendent, John Campbell, called to see me regularly. I felt he may have thought he was putting too much pressure on Sergeant McClelland and I for results.

I resumed work again on 2.2.75 and not long after that, Mr Campbell intimated that I should work from Castlereagh Station. This made things easier as far as travel to and from work was concerned although I was still responsible for the Divisional area. My close friend Sergeant Davy Matthews and I worked continuously in trying to bring together the different religions in Schools, Community Associations, Tenants Associations, Women Together, Youth and Pensioners clubs in all areas and with staff in other Divisions. My ability with the accordion was frequently called on to entertain and we also had some good singers in constable David Grainger, and woman constable Yvonne McKenna from 'B'Division. Brian Lally also acted as M.C. and contributed a lot to these sessions. I was also asked by the Rev. Jimmy Arbuthnot to assist with commentating at the local football matches at Distillery, Glentoran's Oval, Windsor Park and Seaview for Radio Royal, whose broadcasts were relayed to patients in the Royal Victoria Hospital. This I did on a voluntary basis in my own time and quite enjoyed the experience.

It was not long before I was back into the swing of things and with my health improving, I felt things were looking up. Summer camps were organised for youth clubs where we again endeavoured to bring children from each side of the community together. One of these was particularly significant when Davy and I brought Catholic children from the markets area on an outing. While they were away from their area, they were very outgoing and friendly, but it was very noticeable on driving them back into their own area, they increasingly became more hostile and as we left them off, they actually shouted insults at us. This made me think seriously about the influence an area has on its inhabitants.

My daughters, Valerie and Gwendoline had both taken up

employment, Valerie as a nurse in the Ulster Hospital, Dundonald and Gwendoline in the Ulster Bank. By this time, they both had boyfriends and I got a bit of a shock one day when Valerie's boyfriend, Augustus Edgar told me he wanted to marry her and asked for my permission. To me they were still just children and it was the last thing I expected. I began to realise that she in fact was older than I was when I got married so I gave them my blessing. They were married on 19th April, 1976 in the Presbyterian Church on the Ormeau Road with the reception afterwards in La Mons House Hotel. I must say Marie and I thoroughly enjoyed the occasion when all our friends were brought together.

On the morning of 21st June, 1976, the owner of a shop in Upper Dunmurry Lane, Sidney McAvoy was targeted and shot dead by the provisional I.R.A. He, in addition to selling hardware, was a licenced gun dealer from whom the I.R.A. had endeavoured to steal guns in an earlier incident. He in fact had chased them in a car and when they were apprehended at an army check point, gave evidence at their trial which had resulted in their conviction. His killing was obviously aimed at striking terror into those who would give evidence against any members of the organisation. I visited the scene shortly after the murder with W/con McCormick and gave our heartfelt condolences to family relatives and assisted with funeral arrangements.

While there were many atrocities in Northern Ireland throughout 1975 and 1976, the "G" divisional area remained comparatively quiet although our involvement with all of the organisations and bodies involved in community relations meant that we worked long and tedious hours. The Blue Lamp disco, organised and ran by police, was in full swing and constantly in demand from youth clubs throughout the Division. Around the 12th July, 1976, sectarian trouble began to rear its head in the Suffolk/Lenadoon area where a small protestant enclave felt vunerable and were beginning to come under nightly attack. This meant we did not have much time to spend at home with our families. The protestant organisations from the Taughmonagh estate began to come across and organise help for their friends in Suffolk. A confrontation situation developed in which the C.R. Branch played an important part in trying to cool tensions. Both Davy Matthews and Cecil Donald did a lot of good work in bringing sensible people from both areas together and cooling an overheated situation.

On 10th August, 1976, an event occurred which initially had a significant effect on the troubles. An I.R.A unit fired on an army landrover and they gave chase, shooting and killing the driver of the car involved. The car crashed into a family walking along the road and three children were killed. As a result of the wave of revulsion at this incident, the Peace People were formed by an aunt of the children involved, Mairaid Corrigan and another local woman, Betty Williams. Demonstrations of many thousands marched in protest about the troubles and attracted worldwide publicity. However, while the initial reaction was one of condemnation, mainly of the army for shooting the I.R.A. man from the catholic side, and against the I.R.A. on the protestant side, this support to stop the fighting eventually dwindled. Nevertheless, both women received the Novell Peace Prize for their efforts but this again became bathed in controversy. Sir Kenneth Newman had by this time taken over from Sir Jamie Flanagan as Chief Constable and although I suspected at the time this was a political appointment, he had a close and genuine interest in Community Relations. He obviously directed Jack Hermon, his deputy, to keep in touch with what we were doing and Hermon in turn asked me to keep in touch with both women.

On the 25th August, 1976, I received a call to contact the Divisional Commander immediately. Around midday, an I.R.A. unit of four men had attempted to place a bomb on the premises of a Lisburn Road filling station belonging to Mr William Creighton. Mr Creighton bravely grappled with the bombers and one of them shot him dead before making off. A police special patrol group was in the vicinity and made chase after one of the cars used in the bombing. They were chased into Cranmore Gardens off the Malone Road where the gunmen left their vehicle and took a gardener as hostage into a house in the area. They were surrounded by police and a stand off situation developed. The gunmen obviously feared for their lives as they were surrounded by heavily armed police who had lost a lot of comrades to I.R.A. shootings and when speaking contact was made, they requested that father Murphy from Andersonstown be allowed to speak to them first. I went to the scene with Sergeant McClelland and Chief Superintendent Campbell and was involved in getting Father Murphy to come and negotiate with the gunmen. He went into the house and eventually came out with the guns used and the gunmen followed and were taken into custody. As they left the house, I was surprised at the respectable and clean cut appearance of the young men, now murderers, who had just killed a man and bombed a filling station. They were later convicted of the murder and bombing and sentenced to life imprisonment. One of them was to die later on hunger strike.

1977 began with an agreed policy between the Chief Constable Ken Newman and the G.O.C. that police primacy in the rule of law would be the objective. Nevertheless, the level of violence had increased during the first three months of the year and the United Unionist Action Council (UUAC) called a general strike to put pressure on the Government to deal effectively with the Provisional I.R.A. threat. However, the police stood firm in most areas and when the strike began, the trade unions encouraged their members not to support it. The local U.D.A attempted to take over filling stations in the Ravenhill area but this was not permitted and police patrolled the area constantly. Some shops were closed as a result of intimidation but there were plans for the army to take over the power stations if necessary. The police, acting in conjunction with and for the first time controlling the army, cleared many road blocks throughout the province and in East Belfast, where there was face to face confrontations with protestant paramilitaries, they batoned charged and cleared the streets on their own with army support well in the background. The same action was taken following a blockade in Ballymena where a large contingent of police, again backed by army with heavy machinery, showed their intent of relieving the blockade on the town. After a few days, support for the strike dwindled and people began to go back to work. The outcome demonstrated the impartiality of the police in facing up to loyalist gangs of paramilitaries and also suggested they at last were in charge of operations. By this time, my daughter Gwendoline had joined the police and her first station was at Queen Street in Belfast.

On 17th February, 1978, Marie and I were at a Mahee Golf Club prize giving function at Strangford Arms Hotel in Newtownards. Word came through that a huge firebomb had devasted La Mon House Hotel and there were many casualties. We were both very concerned as Marie's brother Eric and his wife Jean had told us they were going to attend a motor cycle club dinner at La Mon that night. We immediately went home and began to telephone friends for news. We were very relieved when we received news from Marie's sister Margaret, that Eric and Jean were safe as they decided for some reason not to go to La Mon. The I.R.A had hung a fire bomb on the protective window grill at one of the restaurants and the resulting fire ball killed twelve people, seven of them women. Thirty other persons were injured and the scene was reported as horrific with pieces of human bodies strewn throughout the hotel, some burned beyond recognition. The I.R.A alleged a warning was given to police but it later transpired that the bomb had gone off before the police could even contact the hotel. This bomb resulted in world wide condemnation of their activities and I was directed to keep in touch with as many organisations as possible in my police area to hammer home the peace message. It was also important to urge restraint in protestant areas so there would be no retaliation.

I was invited by a "G" Division golfing Society to go on a golfing trip to Scotland for a week in March, 1978. I felt I needed a break and it would be good to get away from the pressures of work. I took annual leave and was enjoying a week's golf at courses in Ayrshire, staying at the Naval base in Rosyth. I got a telephone call from my colleague, Davy Matthews, to the effect that I had been transferred to North Queen Street, 'D' Division, to ordinary duty in my absence. I was dumbstruck as no one in Community Relations Branch had mentioned the likelihood of a transfer to me even though I had been in touch with Headquarters just before I went on leave. When I returned to work at Castlereagh, I was summonsed to the Deputy Divisional Commander's office and informed that I was to be transferred to North Queen Street on ordinary duty with effect from 17th April, 1978. It later transpired that the transfer was for my own benefit, but at the time I was extremely annoyed that no one from the branch had given me an inkling that this transfer was in the offing. I did not contact or was I approached by any of my senior officers so I went directly to Central Stores and got fitted out with the necessary uniforms and travelled to North Queen Street on transfer.

In June, 1978, another event occurred which greatly saddened us all. Marie's father, George had been suffering from bouts of asthma and during these attacks he became very breathless. We were staying at the caravan in Ballywalter at the time and I was on duty so Marie drove her father to the Surgery at Lisbane. While George was being treated by the doctor, he suffered a heart attack and was unable to be revived. She was heartbroken and immediately got word to me and to her brother Eric before informing her mother Sarah. The funeral arrangements went ahead and George's passing was a great loss to all of us including his grand-children.

By this time, I had been almost seven years in Community Relations and had lost touch with all the intricacies of ordinary duty. Inspectors were also expected to prosecute in Court and I was somewhat daunted at the prospect of having to stand up and contest cases with experienced solicitors. I will never forget my first day in Court as a prosecutor. Inspector John Young, nicknamed 'The Bull' and who had a huge black beard, was in charge of the court files, about forty of them, and I was expected to go along for experience. I had not seen the files as I was supposed to be there as a spectator to learn. He was selling tickets at the time for the R.U.C. Pipe Band and he left a pile of files, about forty of them, lying on a table in the Court in front of me in complete disarray and said he would be back in a minute. He then began to sell tickets to as many solicitors and court officials as he could. Meanwhile it was getting close to the Court opening and by this time he had disappeared. The Court opened and Mr Jerry Lynn was in charge. The first case was called and the Magistrate addressed me as prosecuting Inspector so I began a frantic search through the dozens of files lying in no particular order in front of me to find the file. I managed to get it and was trying to read through it to find what it was all about when the magistrate asked me for the evidence. I somehow managed to stumble through the case and got a conviction. The same thing happened for the next five or six cases when Inspector Young eventually appeared and took over in his own inimitable way as if there was nothing to get excited about.

When the Court finished, we decided to walk back to North Queen Street via Royal Avenue as it was a lovely sunny day. There we were, two police inspectors in uniform walking along the street and I noticed a girl walking in front of us with very attractive hips. The next thing I knew, the 'Bull' had put his large hand on one of the girl's buttocks and gave it a bit of a shake, at the same time, looking into the girl's face and saying "Lovely morning, isn't it darling"? I was mortified and luckily the girl was so shocked by the big black beard in police uniform staring into her face, she recoiled but didn't do anything about it. This was my introduction to prosecuting at Court and the 'Bull' Young. I learned a couple of very valuable lessons. Number one, meticulous preparation of files before hand and I never appeared in Court again without knowing exactly the make up and evidence and number two, having all files thoroughly researched and in proper sequence before entering the Court. I also learned not to walk out in the street with Inspector Young if it could be avoided. I found there were so many queries and changes of pleas from barristers and solicitors, and if you were not prepared, it was bedlam before a Court started. I began to enjoy the experience after a few weeks and really got into all that I had missed as a uniformed officer.

Duties in North Queen Street included supervision of fixed points at homes of those judges and magistrates who resided in the area. Crusaders football ground, Seaview, was also within the Division and crowd control and movement of spectators to and from matches required a lot of planning and supervision. The 12th July marches also started from the North Queen Street area and there were confrontation points at Tiger Bay and Duncairn Gardens which required to be manned during the eleventh night and twelfth celebrations.

I.P.A. Trip to Matlock

I had joined the International Police Association before going to North Queen Street and in 1978, Chief Inspector Charlie, Boyle and I together with Billy Gillespie decided to form an I.P.A Golfing Society. Superintendent Willie Gray from Mountpottinger was also involved and the idea was to make each outing a social occasion where the society would dress properly in jacket and tie and sit down together for a meal after the golf. Four outings a year were agreed, one each season, and initially there were about sixteen members which has now has risen to forty. This was another outlet to get a break from the continuing murders and mayhem by the I.R.A and protestant paramilitaries. We also managed to arrange a couple of yearly trips to the Arthur Troop Golf Outing in England, one at Matlock in Derbyshire and another at Cheltenham and at the present time the Society has an annual trip to Scotland.

Other stations in the 'D' Divisional area were Greencastle, York road, Fortwilliam, Newtownabbey and Glengormley. An Inspector was attached to each and when they were on leave, I often stood in for them so obtaining a reasonable knowledge of the whole area. I found myself with other police involved in policing loyalist women's protests at Crumlin Road jail and despite the abuse, managed to keep the whole protest of a few days, on a light-hearted basis. Preparation of files for prosecuting at court on a weekly basis and other supervision duties kept me very busy but I was beginning to really enjoy getting back into the relationships of working with a lot of people. Although we worked hard in Community Relations, we felt we were very much on our own and under pressure to come up with results which in the circumstances were well nigh impossible. Now I was beginning to get more job satisfaction from getting results in the areas I was working.

Another surprise awaited me during the second week of August, 1978. I was standing in as Station Inspector for Inspector Laird at North Queen Street when I received a telephone call from Chief

Superintendent Harry McCullough from Headquarters, offering me promotion to the rank of Chief Inspector and a transfer to Newry in 'H' Division. There was one proviso, that I was required to move house to the general area. This was surprising because police were beginning to move away from the Newry area because of the increased threat from terrorists. I told him I would discuss it with my wife and let him know my decision. I went home and talked it over with Marie and although it meant another upheaval for the family, we decided we would move. I rang Mr McCullough and told him I would accept the promotion and move to Banbridge. This was acceptable and I said my farewells to all the friends I had made in North Queen Street and on 1st September, 1978, I moved on transfer as Chief Inspector to Newry, on appointment as Deputy Sub-Divisional Commander.

Corry Square Station, Newry

Chapter 8
(Newry)

My first meeting was to be with my immediate boss, the Sub Divisional Commander, Superintendent Paddy Maguire. I went to Newry Station, Corry Square, and my first impressions were that it was a bit of a tip. It was an old two storied building at the corner of Catherine Street and Edward Street with a large number of small rooms which needed re-painting and initial impressions were anything but good. The public area was small and the Station Sergeant's office was conveniently sited at the rear of the guardroom. At the top of the stairs, the Sub-divisional Commander's office was on the right and as Newry was a Divisional Headquarters at the time, the Divisional commander's office was along the corridor to the left and the divisional clerk's office immediately opposite. My office was along the corridor to the right, opposite the radio control room.

The Station Sergeant at that time was Fred Bratton who had followed a real character called Billy Junk, but Fred made his own mark in Newry as an astute and sensitive policeman who was very much in touch with both the Nationalist and Unionist people. At the top of the stairs was a black marble memorial with the names of those officers who had been murdered by terrorists but I did not foresee that in my time in the Division, a further large black marble tablet would be necessary to hold all the names of those officers who were to make the supreme sacrifice.

When Marie and I went to the Station we were directed to the Superintendent's office. Paddy was a tall gangly man with a shock of brown hair who towered over us and greeted us warmly. He leaned back in his chair after getting us seated and with his huge smile and easy going attitude made us both feel completely at ease. I felt very much at home and then Paddy took us on a tour of the station. While the accommodation was sparse, the morale

Roll of Honour Newry Sub-Division

Constable T C J Gregg	4th July 1957
Constable H B Ross	16th July 1958
Constable W J Hunter	12th November 1961
Constable S Donaldson	12th August 1970
Constable R Millar	12th August 1970
Sergent T R Morrow	2nd March 1972
Constable S R D Houston	26th June 1972
Constable G M Rolston	11th December 1973
Constable T G McCall	16th April 1974
Constable D J A McNeice	14th December 1974
Sergeant J Hunter	15th May 1976
Constable H McConnell	17th June 1978
Constable W H Turbitt	17th June 1978
Constable R A Baird	17th April 1979
Constable P M Gray	17th April 1979
Reserve Constable R A Lockhart	17th April 1979
Constable N A Webb	17th April 1979
Superintendent S Hanna	3rd June 1979
Constable K Thompson	3rd June 1979
Constable K J Acheson	2nd April 1981
Constable M B Robinson	27th May 1981
Constable N Quinn	20th June 1981
Sergeant E Brown	6th January 1983
Reserve Constable B A Quinn	6th January 1983
Reserve Constable W E Magill	20th February 1983
Reserve Constable F T Morton	15th March 1983
Reserve Constable W R Fullerton	10th January 1984
Sergeant W R Savage	31st January 1984
Constable T J Bingham	31st January 1984

Constable W N Gray	18th May 1984
Reserve Constable T G Elliott	18th May 1984
Sergeant J F C Murphy	21st February 1985
Chief Inspector A Donaldson	28th February 1985
Detective Sergeant J T Dowd	28th February 1985
Detective W/Constable I W Kelly	28th February 1985
W/Constable R E McGookin	28th February 1985
Constable D P Topping	28th February 1985
Reserve Constable D A Price	28th February 1985
Reserve Constable P H McFerran	28th February 1985
Reserve Constable S B McHenry	28th February 1985
Reserve Constable G K Campbell	28th February 1985
Reserve Constable M K Kay	3rd April 1985
Inspector W J Wilson	20th May 1985
W/Constable T E Doak	20th May 1985
Constable D J R Baird	20th May 1985
Reserve Constable S G Rodgers	20th May 1985
Constable D Hanson	15th November 1985
Constable D L McBride	22nd May 1986
Constable W L Smith	22nd May 1986
Sergeant P J Kilpatrick	26th July 1986
Constable T W C Allen	26th July 1986
Constable K C Blackbourne	26th July 1986
C/Superintendent H A Breen	20th March 1989
Superintendent R J Buchannan	20th March 1989
Constable M F L Marshall	20th October 1989
Detective Constable L M Robinson	15th September 1990
W/Constable C L McMurray	27th March 1992
Constable J Reid	25th February 1993
Reserve Constable B J W Woods	2nd November 1993

of the people we met appeared to be high, everyone was warm and friendly and the kitchen staff and cleaners went about their business in a cheery manner. The general noise of the station gave a good impression as the policemen and women were whistling and singing as they changed shifts and moved about from room to room and getting on with their duties generally. At this stage, there was little outside protection other than a high chain link wire fence with a sanger at the corner that had a view of both Edward Street and Catherine Street. We left the station with a much better feeling than when we first arrived and I felt we would be happy there once we had settled in and moved house.

During the first week, Paddy took me round the other Sub Division Stations, Bessbrook, Warrenpoint, Newtownhamilton, Rathfriland, Forkhill and Crossmaglen. I met all of the Sergeants and some of the Constables who were on duty at the time. Some of the men I met on my first week were later murdered by the provisional I.R.A. They were experienced men, concerned with policing in their area and in particular, the welfare of the communities they served. They were in touch with the dangers and obviously related closely to the Sub Divisional Commander. I have since come to respect Paddy Maguire as one of the better officers in the R.U.C, a very capable officer who should have progressed but I'm unsure whether he had been deliberately overlooked for promotion or had simply refused to be considered for higher rank. I was introduced to Inspectors Gerry Davidson, Felix Duffy and Sam Martin who I was to work closely with during the next few years. Inspectors Harry Walker and Errol McDowell were attached to Bessbrook station and both had working experience in the Newry area and South Armagh area and the advice I got from these men was invaluable. Inspectors Kevin Burns, Phil Baron and Paddy Doyle were later to arrive and Inspectors Jack Middleton was in charge of Newtownhamilton, Henry McMullan in Crossmaglen later to be succeeded by Bob Green and Alan McQuillan, and Bob Foster in Forkhill.

A number of military personnel were installed in Newry Station for protection duties and joint patrolling. They generally were there for a four month period and while there were a number of good officers, their training was not the same as a police officer. Very often, in a joint Police/Army patrol where police primacy was important, a strong minded army N.C.O. could take over and people sympathetic to the police, were dissuaded by the aggressive questioning and intelligence gathering attitude of the military. Subsequent events shaped my attitude that Newry town, Warrenpoint and Rathfriland should be policed by police alone with military in a support role manning static protection points and vehicle check points around each of these areas as required, particularly on the border side with the Irish Republic. We were grateful for the assistance of the Royal Military Police who were also deployed throughout Newry but it was important to get through to them that the population should not be treated as squaddies.

I was only five days into my transfer to Newry when I was initiated into the viciousness of I.R.A. terrorism. In September, 1978, Billy McAlpine, a family man who worked in the bacon factory was driving home for his lunch along Chapel Street when a gunmen stepped out from behind a telegraph pole and opened fire. The car crashed into the pole at the gates of St Mary's Church and it was alleged the gunmen ran over and fired further shots into his head. I arrived at the scene within minutes in the district car and found Mr McAlpine's lifeless body lying half out of the door of his car, his head which had been shattered by the high velocity shots, on the road and his brains oozing along the gutter. I immediately preserved the scene and radioed for scenes of crime officers. It transpired that Mr McAlpine was a major in the Army Cadet Force, a voluntary organisation which got a number of boys from both religions together and gave them some outdoor activity. The I.R.A later tried to justify this heinous crime by suggesting he was part of the 'British War Machine'. This was a cowardly attack on a decent man and a soft target. It angers me that those responsible still walk the streets of Dundalk.

A further two murders were committed by the same terrorist unit with the next couple of weeks. Later in September, Joe Skelly was a passenger in his son in law's car who had been a member of the R.U.C Reserve. Again, like Billy McAlpine, they were on their way home for lunch from the Industrial Estate in Greenbank when they were fired on from another car in Quay Street then in Lower William Street. Both men had been hit but their car broke down as they tried to escape and they were fired on again in River Street and William Street as they were trying to get to Daisy Hill Hospital. Joe Skelly was killed in this attack and his son-in-law wounded in the back. A few days later, in October, a local farmer, Charlie Henning, unarmed, was selling livestock at the Newry market. As he was leaving and about to enter his lorry he saw the gunmen approaching and ran back towards the market. They ran after him and shot him a number of times. He died later in Daisy Hill Hospital. Charlie was a part-time Major in the U.D.R and after his death, I attended the wake at his home another very sad occasion.

All three of these decent law-abiding men were unarmed soft targets and I have nothing but contempt for the murderers who caused their deaths and who professed to be fighting for freedom in Ireland. On 21st December, an army foot patrol was on duty in the square, Crossmaglen. An innocent looking post-office van drove into the square. The back doors opened and heavy automatic gunfire raked the first four members of the patrol, killing three before making off. Fire was returned but no hits claimed. Another cowardly attack leaving three brave young men dead.

Meanwhile, Marie and I had been looking for a house in Banbridge and we decided to buy a new one at Harberton Park on the Ballygowan Road. The house was not yet completed so we looked for suitable accommodation in Banbridge. My son Gary was six years old at the time and he probably looked on this as a great adventure although he had to leave his friends at Rathmore School in Bangor. Early in 1979, we managed to get rented accommodation in a flat over the Windsor Bakery and Gary still recalls the smell of baking bread every morning when he and his mother went down to the bakery to get doughnuts. There was a heavy snow fall that year and about six inches of water which had been lying in the bath in the flat was frozen solid. Gary recalls urinating in the toilet and because of the steam rising due to the freezing cold, thought there was something wrong with him. He continued his education at Banbridge Primary School where he made new friends quite quickly, his closest being Stephen Rourke. The snow fall that year was such that the mini we were driving at the time was fully covered in the snow. We intended to go to Australia to visit my daughter Valerie and my brother Wallace and I had saved all my annual leave for 1978. The new leave year started in April, 1979, and I used it together with the saved leave to have two months well earned holiday.

On 1st March, 1979 Marie, Gary and I set off for Australia. My daughters Gwendoline and Carol had already travelled out to visit their sister and were in Australia when we arrived. Gwendoline came home on her own and Carol had a job and intended to come home with us. We had a great time enjoying the sunny weather in Sydney but after a huge meal with a couple of friends from Bathhurst, we were travelling back to my daughter's house by train and I took a terrible pain in the chest. I realised I was having my second heart attack and I was taken to Ryde Hospital where it was confirmed. I spent ten days in the hospital and while I was there, in April, 1979, Newry had another tragedy. Four of my colleagues from Bessbrook were killed in a land rover when a huge van bomb exploded as they drove past. It had been hi-jacked that morning. I was anxious to find out who they were and the Sydney police got in touch with Newry and I received a telegram to the hospital from the Divisional commander, Paddy McCullough, confirming that Constables Alan Baird, Paul Gray,

Noel Webb and Robert Lockhart had all been killed. I had known each of these men personally and I was devastated to hear this dreadful news.

My daughter Gwendoline was still serving as a WPC in Queen Street and had decided she met the love of her life in Neil Fraser, a police constable who had served in the army so she informed me that she was going to get married. I asked her if she was sure she met the right man and she assured me she had. I thereby gave her my blessing and they were married in April. Gwen left the force shortly after to become a full-time housewife and Neil and Gwen have since raised a family of five, four girls and one boy, Natasha, Trudy, Carly, Kathy and Jonathan. They are all great children and Marie and I as grand parents are very proud of them all.

We had intended to take a further holiday in Queensland for a week but when I left hospital, I was in no position to go so it was cancelled. Neither would the doctors give me permission to return home immediately because of my condition so I remained in Sydney for another two months before I was allowed to fly home. During my time on sick leave, two incidents occurred, one of which led to the greatest loss of life the army had yet sustained. In June, Superintendent Stanley Hanna and Constable Kevin Thompson were walking along the road near Silverbridge assisting in an army search operation. A huge bomb concealed in a milk churn at the side of the road exploded killing both instantly. The bomb had been detonated by a radio controlled device. Stanley had been appointed Border Superintendent, the same job I was later to do, with a brief to control operations around the border and liaise with the Gardai. He was a personal friend and also a member of the International Police Association. As I was a founder member of the number two region I.P.A. Golf Society, we decided to play for a cup yearly in his honour and the Stanley Hanna Memorial Trophy is played for each year on our annual trip to Scotland. I was fortunate to be part of the team who won it on a couple of occasions.

I was still on sick leave when two roadside bombs were left by the Provisional I.R.A. at a lay-by on the dual carriageway near Warrenpoint. One exploded as a truck load of soldiers passed killing a number of personnel. As they set up an incident centre convenient to the explosion, another bomb, a secondary device, which had been planted with the intention to kill, exploded killing more personnel. In all, eighteen soldiers lost their lives including Lieutenant Colonel, David Blair. On the same day, a bomb set in a boat in County Sligo killed Lord Louis Mountbatten and two young boys. It was alleged by Eamon Collins that Brendan Burns was responsible for the explosions at Warrenpoint and Burns later died when a bomb he was making exploded prematurely.

Meanwhile, I was anxious to get back to work and had recovered reasonably well but was afraid that my authorities might transfer me back to an office job in Belfast. I was anxious to remain in Newry and intimated this to the Chief Medical Officer of the force, Dr Hagan. He was a very decent man and although he had some misgivings about it, he respected my wishes and allowed me to return to full-time duties in Newry. After a long period on sick leave I resumed duty on 17th September, 1979 and it was not long before the next murder by the I.R.A took place. George Hawthorne who had been a member of the U.D.R. but had left the regiment the previous year, was shot dead by gunmen from a car in Soho car park. I attended the funeral of Mr Hawthorne and offered my condolences to his family.

In addition to supervision and other duties in Newry, as a Chief Inspector, I was regularly called upon by Complaints and Discipline Branch to investigate complaints against lower ranks in any part of the province. The Branch was snowed under by frivolous complaints orchestrated by the P.I.R.A. propaganda machine so officers outside the Branch were called upon to assist. A lot of time was spent on such investigations in surrounding areas such as Portadown and Armagh. I also attended numerous meetings with the then South Down representative at Westminster, the Right

Honourable Enoch Powell in relation to late night " burger bar" trading in Warrenpoint which he was obviously being harassed about by other traders with an axe to grind. I considered these to be trivial matters which should be dealt with by the local council enforcement officer and that police should only be involved if there was a breach of the peace. I told him so but he was of the opinion that the police should be involved so we took up different positions. He also complained of speeding in the area which I agreed was a police matter and I discussed this with local police and a good friend in the traffic branch in Armagh, Chief Inspector Joe Elliot, in an attempt to curb the speeding offences. I explained to Mr Powell that because of the terrorist threat against police, it was difficult to maintain a high profile of traffic policing duties in the area which I believe he understood.

During the month of January, 1980, there were numerous demonstrations in Newry protesting about the removal of political status from prisoners and following these demonstrations, a spate of fire bombings on commercial premises in the town. One of these attacked was Cahill's shop in the town centre and Hoggs Travel Agents shop was also attacked by incendiaries. The disorder was on a nightly basis and a fire bomb attack on the Ulsterbus Depot, left eleven buses destroyed and three badly damaged. In March there was a bomb attack on Crossmaglen Station and luckily no one was injured. I attended the scene with Superintendent Ossie Dixon by helicopter and arranged to have the Department of Enviroment replace windows which had been smashed in some of the surrounding private houses. Our Divisional Commander, Paddy McCullagh was transferred to Headquarters and was replaced by Chief Superintendent Sam McFarland who I had served with in Dunmurry. I knew Sam personally as a dedicated and sensible policeman and knew that the Division was still in safe hands.

In March, 1980, an I.R.A unit attacked the custom post at Newry with the intention of destroying it. Robert Carr was one of the unit and the firebomb he was carrying exploded prematurely and he was engulfed in a ball of fire. His so-called 'heroic' comrades ran off over the border leaving him to his own devices and subsequent reports from some of those involved suggest that he discarded his clothes and made his way to a near-by house and was taken to a hospital in County Louth where he died on 1st April, 1980. I attended at his funeral in a supervisory capacity which took place on 4th April. It was a difficult one as far as supervision was concerned as the remains were brought to Newry from Dublin the previous evening and there was concern that an I.R.A display might take place over the coffin. A heavy police presence was necessary to prevent this although they did get some publicity by staging something at the house on the evening before the funeral.

Warrenpoint had been comparatively quiet over this particular period but in April, the police station came under mortar attack. The station was immediately evacuated and army bomb disposal squad tasked to search for unexploded mortars. Again, there were no serious injuries and I arranged for a temporary mobile station and canteen to be set up and asked for addition help from District Mobile Support units from Portadown and Armagh and to have the Department of Enviroment arrange to board-up civilian windows in the vicinity.

The next attempt to kill policemen took place at Newtownhamilton. Four policemen were travelling in an armoured car on the Newtownhamilton/Newry Road when a huge landmine went off on the roadside as they passed. They were all injured, Sergeant Stewart Johnston suffered a fractured skull, cracked ribs and a dislocated hip joint, Constable Trevor Cartmill received bruising to face and ribs and a broken ankle, Constable Davis had facial bruising and shock and R/Constable McMurray had facial bruising and shock. The armoured car was completely destroyed but had in fact saved the lives of all concerned. It would appear that whoever was on the firing point of this landmine also got the timing slightly wrong. I went to the scene immediately with

Superintendent Dixon and the ambulance had already arrived. The injured men were conveyed to Daisyhill Hospital. An armed guard was arranged at the Hospital and I called to see them that evening. Sergeant Johnston was transferred to the Royal Victoria where I again called with him the following evening.

Since I moved to Banbridge, I decided to join Warrenpoint Golf Club so I put in an application and was accepted. There I met many of the local businessmen and built up a very good local knowledge and insight of the area. It was a difficult to arrange any sort of regular golf at week-ends because of the security situation as I would have been easily targeted, so I never made any arrangements to play on a regular basis. I just went down quietly and had a quick round now and again. Most of the people I came in contact with at the club had my welfare in mind and I believe looked after me. I made many friends and really enjoyed my time there. In my limited spare time I was still playing golf with the R.U.C. Golfing Society and with the I.P.A. Golf Society.

Welfare Committee, Newry

While there had been horrific incidents, Warrenpoint was still an area which did not participate much in the hatefilled rantings of other areas and both religions still lived in relative harmony. However, at week-ends, there was an influx of a noisier type crowd from the South Armagh area which often resulted in disorderly conduct. The local Sergeant, Mick Maguire, lived in the town for a long time and had his finger on the pulse. He was well known and the people had great respect for him and indeed looked after him for many years as he did them. However, the threat from the I.R.A. became so intense that he was eventually forced to move to Banbridge to the consternation of most of the residents of the town.

Shortly after arrival at Newry, I was appointed chairman of a voluntary welfare group which consisted of a small committee which looked after widows and pensioners in the area. We organised trips and functions where they could get together and mull over times past. Each of the stations in the sub-division was represented and very active members of the committee were Sergeant Matt Gilmore and Cyril Simpson from Bessbrook, Herbie Fullerton and W/Sergeant Rosie Todd and Allison from Newry. . Herbie was my Sub Divisional clerk and a very dependable person. During my time as Chairman, I met interesting people. One former County Inspector was 'Dusty Ferris' who had a reputation as an over strict disciplinarian when he was serving but I found him to be a charming man, living in Rostrevor, whose wife was severely disabled and he attended to her ever need without assistance. He really enjoyed our visits when he could chat about policing and old times. Ex District Inspector O'Brien who had written many text books to help budding police officers with their studies, also lived in Warrenpoint and looked forward to my visits.

Another great character was ex District Inspector Jack Shea. An unmarried man, when he retired from the R.U.C. he decided he wanted to see the world and took up the position of purser on a ship. He travelled the world for a few years and finally bought a house convenient to Derrybeg, a working class housing estate in Newry. It says a lot for the character of the man when an ex R.U.C. officer could survive in such an area at that time. He got involved with the local Community association which was probably close to the Official I.R.A. and acted as spokesman for them in any dealings with the police in relation to inquiries about relatives interned etc. His family were initially from the south of Ireland where his father had been in the Royal Irish Constabulary. He often related to me in a humorous way that they were continually harassed in the South because they were an R.I.C. family with links to the crown so when the R.I.C. was disbanded, his father joined the R.U.C. and moved to Rathfriland , they were harassed because they were Catholic. Jack was a huge rotund man with a great sense of humour and you would recognize his hearty laugh in any company. He was always called upon to perform the song 'the laughing policeman' at functions he attended which had everyone in stiches because of his infectious laugh. Jack's brother Paddy was also a high ranking official in the civil service. My third daughter, Carol, by this time had decided she wanted to serve in the Royal Ulster Constabulary and when she completed her training, moved to Donegal Pass Station.

1981 began with another cowardly murder by the provisional I.R.A. In January, Ivan Toombs, a customs official was in his office in Warrenpoint dockyard when two men on a motorbike free-wheeled into the yard. They went to his office and opened fire on him at point blank range, killing him instantly. Ivan was a major in the Ulster Defence Regiment in his spare time and was a hard-working family man who had worked unceasingly for the community. Eamon Collins, also a customs official, later admitted his part in targeting Ivan Toombs and gave information as to who had committed the murder but later retracted his statement after pressure from the Provisionals. I attended the scene of the murder with Chief Superintendent McFarland and set in motion the preservation of the scene and search for the vehicle used. I later went and spoke to the family and attended the funeral at Warrenpoint Parish Church in uniform which was a very sad affair. Constable Kenny Acheson finished his shift at Bessbrook Station on 2nd April, 1981 around 11pm. He went to his car which was parked near-by and drove off. As he drove along the road a device exploded underneath the car which killed him instantly. Kenny was a young married constable with an eleven month old child and a great loss to his family, the community, and particularly to his colleagues in Bessbrook.

In the middle of this mayhem which we were all experiencing at work, my father Tommy, complained a bit about chest pains but no one took his complaints too seriously. He went to a Boys Brigade re-union in March and he was in great form, meeting all his former colleagues and having a great time. He suddenly collapsed, fell on the floor and never uttered another word. It transpired he had a huge anurism when the aorta valve connected to the heart ruptured. He was probably dead before he touched the floor. I was informed by a cousin, Willie Cunningham, who contacted me before informing my mother. This was a hugely sad occasion and by the time the funeral arrangements were made and all the relatives informed the funeral was on us before we realised it. My brother Wallace flew home from Australia and delivered the eulogy at the service. I was particularly sad because my father and I were close and I felt that my son Gary who was still comparatively young, had lost both his grand-fathers within a very short period of time.

The first hunger strike finished in December, 1981 after negotiations between representatives of the British Government and the I.R.A. prisoners in Long Kesh. The prisoners thought their demands had been met when in fact they had not. One of those on hunger strike was Sean McKenna whose family lived in Newry. When he came off the hunger strike, I was sent to the family to inform them that he had come off the hunger strike. I was rather apprehensive as to what reception to expect. I was surprised in that I was met at the door by a very good looking girl, possibly his sister and I was invited into a very clean and tidy house and treated with the utmost respect by his sister and parents. They were obviously delighted that he had come off the hunger strike but I suspect they had already heard the news on the grapevine from Father Faul who had campaigned vigorously at that time on behalf of the prisoners. They thanked me for letting them know.

When the hunger strike proper began, police were under pressure in all Catholic areas because of the street demonstrations and disorder orchestrated by the provisional I.R.A. There was the usual instances of black humour and I remember being at a football match at the Oval when Glentoran were playing a foreign team in the U.F.F.A. Cup when one glentoran wag shouted, "Come on Glentoran, Bobby Sands could eat that team." There were the usual Easter parades, one Official and one Provisional, which had to be supervised and extra police were brought into the town by way of District Mobile Support Units. Luckily, these passed off with only minor incidents and a cycle race was also supervised. The Sub Divisional Commander, Paddy Maguire, retained a reserve of police in the station until things had quietened down. I was worried about the security of one of my constables Mervyn Robinson. He lived in South Armagh and I was aware there had been a number of protestants killed in the area. I spoke to him and implored him to move house to a safer area but he and his wife Martha were adamant that the family would not move. I asked him to at least consider his position and have an alarm installed at his house. He agreed and this was done on 1st May.

In May, an illegal parade in support of the hunger strikers took place in Monaghan Street. I attended with a number of police and gave the verbal warning that the parade was illegal with the intention of summonsing the organisers at a later date. They set off and marched via Monaghan Street, Merchants Quay, Sugar Island, Water Street, William Street, John Mitchel Place to Marcus Square. They held a meeting at Marcus Square and after the meeting about thirty to forty youths broke away and commenced stone throwing at police. I ordered police to don riot gear and start walking towards them with shields and baton and the youths dispersed without baton rounds being fired. More stone throwing took place at Barcroft Park but these were also dispersed and two arrests made. These types of incidents were occurring on a regular basis and in addition to all the every day policing duties, added to what was already overstretched police duties. Appeals for more police man-power for the sub-division generally fell on deaf ears.

Again following the death of the hunger striker, Bobby Sands on 5th May, trouble erupted throughout the Division. Police went on to twelve hour shifts and indeed longer hours were worked when needed. Unfortunately, our own Divisional Mobile patrols were called to Belfast to deal with disturbances and we were very much left to our own devices with a skeleton staff to cope with anything with might occur. When Raymond McCreesh from Camlough, the third hunger striker died, I went to the house and told the family that the body would be brought straight home with a police escort to prevent any coat-trailing throughout the town to raise feelings. I was not very well received but managed to get the message through. McCreesh had been serving a sentence for conspiracy to murder soldiers and membership of the I.R.A. and was involved in a shooting incident with soldiers when he was captured. Because feelings in Catholic areas were in sympathy with the deaths from the hunger strike, everyone in the police service in Newry was very much aware of the heightened threat and their personal security.

On May,19th, a huge bomb was detonated under a Saracen armoured vehicle near Camlough killing five soldiers from the Royal Green Jackets regiment. The bomb had been dug into a culvert and was detonated by a radio controlled device from some distance away. There was some suggestion at the time that the bomb had been of similar construction to those which had killed soldiers at Warrenpoint and attempts were made to have Brendan

Burns, the well known I.R.A. bomb maker, extradicted to answer charges. However the procedure was unsuccessful but Burns later died when a bomb he was making exploded prematurely, some might say poetic justice. Eamon Collins again had knowledge of those from Newry who dug in the command wire and detonated the explosion which resulted in the deaths of the five young soldiers.

Near the end of May, Constable Mervyn Robinson was shot dead as he left the local bar only about 200 yards from his house. The murderers were in a car and opened fire on an unarmed man as he left the pub. It particularly distressed me as I had implored Mervyn and his wife Martha to move house. When I called at the house after his death, Martha said, "you're wee alarm didn't do much good." Mervyn had lived in the area all his life and in the past had actually socialised in the same pub with many of the local youth who he must have suspected were involved in I.R.A. activities but believed that they would not have harmed him. In a later conversation with Eugene Reavey, the brother of the Reavey Brothers shot dead in 1976 by the U.V.F. including rogue members of the security forces, Eugene told me that Paddy Quinn, his brother in law, who was well known to Mervyn and had been in prison at the time for I.R.A. offences, actually cried when he heard that Mervyn had been shot. I assisted with the funeral arrangements, took the Chief Constable to the house and attended Mervyn's funeral on 30th May. Two policewomen, Margaret Sturdy and Irene Thompson sang 'One day at a time' at the service at the request of Mervyn's wife Martha.

On the last day of May, I was duty officer in Newry when called to a suspect car at Drumalane. When I arrived, the duty Inspector had already called the army bomb disposal team and had sealed off an area about 200 yards on either side of the suspect car. The army bomb disposal officer, Michael O,Neill, had already looked at the car and came back to the incident centre where I was standing. He told me he had checked most of the car out

Secretary of State visit, Newry

and everything seemed O.K but he was still not sure about the glove compartment. He went back to the car and after he entered it there was a huge explosion. We rushed to the remains of the car and found Michael's body lying about twenty yards from the disintegrated car, obviously dead. His arm had been decapitated from his body and some of the local residents came out and were most obviously distressed. I knew that Michael was of the Roman Catholic faith so I went to the local chapel to ask for a priest to come and speak over the body. After some persuasion, I managed to get one of them to come along and say a few words. Eamon Collins later described in his book 'Killing Rage' the details of what happened and his dealings with 'Brian' who had set the explosive charge in the glove compartment of the car which killed Michael O'Neill. Apparently a photo electric cell was used to set off the bomb when exposed to light.

Constable Neal Quinn was looking forward to his retirement

from the R.U.C. at the end of June. He had a plain clothes job in looking after compensation claims and was having a quiet drink at lunch time in Mick Toner's pub, 'The Bridge Bar, on 20th June, when two provisional I.R.A. killers in motor cycle gear walked in and shot him dead at point blank range. The killers then ran out and made good their escape. I called with Mrs Quinn who was devastated and helped with the funeral arrangements and attended the funeral together with other police officers. Eamon Collins also described in his book how he assisted with the targeting of Neal Quinn and knew those who carried out the murder. Constables Campbell and Lockhart were on mobile patrol near the Mountainview pub in July.. When they were in the act of passing a parked car it exploded and they were both injured, though fortunately not life threatening. Both were taken to Daisyhill Hospital in Newry where I visited them that evening. Luckily the attempt to murder them was slightly mistimed, otherwise there would have been two more fatalities.

Around the beginning of August, 1981, there were numerous terrorist attacks by way of bombing filling stations, hi-jacking cars, bombing railway lines between Newry and the border. Hunger strikers were continuing to die and protests took place on a daily basis keeping policing in the area stretched to breaking point and in September, there was an attempted mortar attack on Bessbrook Station. Protest marches were continuing and policing these events were exhausting, both mentally and physically for the police in the Newry area. Towards the end of September, an annual Apprentice Boys parade, (a protestant organisation) was due to take place, starting from Monaghan Street and we found out through the grapevine that an "H" block protest march had been arranged to take place from the same venue at exactly the same time. I was first informed by a member of Sinn Fein that the H Block march would be a half hour later than the apprentice boys. I was told later that some of the hard liners arranging the march had changed the time to co-incide with the apprentice boys parade and that the sinn fein member who had informed me of the different times was annoyed and had made attempts to contact me to let me know the change in times.

I had already taken action to have police positioned so there would be no confrontations as it would have caused enormous problems and one that we could not allow to happen. Discussions began, and with some difficulty, times were changed to allow about half an hour between the parades and routes were suggested to keep both section apart. A huge police presence was necessary as there were elements on both sides looking for confrontation but through careful monitoring of the situation we managed to keep the parades separated by manning the bridges over the Newry river. There was some concern for the safety of my immediate boss, Paddy Maguire, as he still resided in the Newry area and was a prime target. He was therefore transferred to Headquarters and I acted as sub-divisional commander for the next few months. The deputy Divisional Commander, Ossie Dixon was also replaced by Archie Hayes around this time.

Ben Dunne a well known business man who was the managing director of Dunnes stores which traded both north and south of the border, was driving his Mercedes car on the road between Dundalk and Newry in October when he was stopped and kidnapped by a number of armed men. His car was left on the road-side with the keys in the ignition. This was a very expensive car and when I arrived on the scene I had a cursory look over the car for bobby traps, then got in touch with the manager of Dunnes stores in Dundalk. He came along and also had a look over the car. We felt everything was in order so I got in and drove it to Newry Station where it was held for forensic examination. Ben Dunne was held for a few days and later released. There was no ransom request that was known to police but I have no information as to whether the Dunne family were approached directly or if a ransom was paid or not.

The next day was another shock for Marie and I. Her sister

Margaret told us that her mother Sarah had died suddenly. Sarah had been living with Margaret for some time and while we knew she was not very well, her death was completely unexpected. She found it very difficult to get over her husband George's passing and Marie and I were glad we had spent a few days with her on a cruiser on the Fermanagh Lakes about a month before she died. She had really enjoyed the short holiday and spoke about it often. The usual arrangements had to be made and a large number of friends and relatives attended the wake and the funeral to Comber graveyard.

Sammy Hamilton, a part time member of the R.U.C.R. was leaving his employment from the Housing Executive Offices at the rear of Newry Cathedral in November. As he left the office, he was struck down by automatic gunfire and was taken to Daisy Hill Hospital. This was a cold blooded murder attempt and a Hi Ace van left in the vicinity was suspected to be the vehicle involved. I arranged for military to examine the vehicle in case of booby trap devices and the following evening, I visited Mrs Hamilton at her home to express my concern at the attempted murder of her husband and if there was anything we could do to help her in the circumstances.

The year 1981 ended in dealing with floods in Kilmorey Street, Newry, by arranging sandbags, and with a bomb in Henry Thompson's liquor store in Greenbank Industrial estate in which the terrorists parked their getaway car in Chapel Hill. I was in charge at the scene with other police and was suspicious of the car on this occasion so I arranged for the military to get bomb disposal along. Luckily, my suspicions were correct as the car was booby trapped with a large bomb in the boot which the bomb disposal team disposed off with a large explosion. I was also concerned about the safety of some of the Unionist members of Newry District Council because of the heightened security threat and spoke to each of them about their personal safety and the need to change routes and cars and to be constantly aware of the dangers. In December, Billy Howard arrived to replace Paddy Maguire as Sub Divisional Commander.

1982 began with our Divisional Commander, Sam McFarland being replaced by Keith Farlow. There were incidents of bombs on the railway line, armed robberies in Jonesboro and Drumintee post offices and in the Roxboro Café in Newry. A bomb was placed in the Crown Hotel in Warrenpoint and it was tragic to see such an old historic building which was the heart of the town completely destroyed. Unsuccessful attempts were also made to bomb the Rockfoot Filling Station on the Belfast Road. One of our constables, George Dickson, was engaged in stopping traffic on the Dublin Road when he was unfortunately struck by a car and fatally injured. Bombs were also placed at Newry Golf Club and when Sergeant Stubber and I attended and set up a command post at the junction of Forkhill Road, Dublin Road, the Sergeant jumped over a stone wall only to land on a secondary device which had been placed to kill police. Fortunately it did not explode and was defused by the army bomb squad. This was one of a number of occasions in which we were lucky not to be numbered as fatalities.

Notwithstanding the demands placed on police by terrorism, we were still under pressure to continue the everyday running of a police station in dealing with the ordinary people. The investigation of normal complaints, the ordinary run of the mill crimes such as burglary and theft and the escorting of explosives from the Republic of Ireland through the sub-division all had to be dealt with on an every day basis. We had at this time at our disposal a District Mobile Support Unit (DMSU) which consisted of an Inspector, Four Sergeants, and twenty four Constables in four landrovers which we could deploy and I was anxious to deploy South of Newry to keep checks on the southern roads used by the terrorists to attack the town. However, Paisley's protestant 'third force' began to cause problems around this time so the DMSU was often diverted away from the Division to keep an eye out for them instead of being able to do the job against IRA terrorism.

Easter 1982 saw the expected parades from the Provisional I.R.A and the Official I.R.A. take place in the town. About six hundred people and three bands attended the provisional parade which took place in the morning and the Official parade of about three hundred and two bands started at midday. Both passed off without incident although there was some cat calling between spectators. A world championship fishing competition had also been organised to take place in Newry and teams from all over the world were scheduled to arrive. It was important for Newry Chamber of Commerce and Newry District Council to see this event through without too much trouble so as to attract tourism to the area. This also became another security headache as the bombings and shootings in the Newry/South Armagh area had been well publicised throughout the world. Apprentice Boys parades were also supervised in Rathfriland where thirty six bands, about two thousand apprentice boys and around three thousand spectators took part. A bomb hoax in the sale yard in Rathfriland caused some delay to this parade until it was cleared by army bomb disposal.

Because of the hectic pace and pressure of policing Newry at that time, it was important to get away now and again on sports leave. We were entitled to two days each month but were seldom able to avail of them because of constant incidents at work. However, on 14th June I was able to play in the mixed foursomes golf tournament organised by the R.U.C. Golfing Society at Royal Belfast. I was playing with John Connor, a constable from Headquarters, his wife Margaret and a friend of hers named Phylis. It was a lovely sunny day and I was enjoying my golf. When we reached the seventh hole which was an uphill par three of about one hundred and eighty yards, I played a four iron and hit what appeared to be a good shot. Suddenly, the four ball in front of us who were standing on the eight tee above the seventh green began to shout and wave their arms in the air. I wondered what they were doing and suddenly realised they must have seen my ball

115

going into the hole for a 'hole in one'. This was confirmed by Wally Cunningham as he came down the hill. This was my first hole in one and at the prize giving, the Chief Constable, Jack Hermon, with his warped sense of humour, made some caustic remark about those who could get a hole in one must have been playing too much golf. I remember thinking of the long hours I had worked and all the mates I had lost and that this ass hole sitting in Headquarters was well out of touch to make such a comment.

I was brought back to earth again shortly after this when Albert White was shot dead in front of his wife. Albert was a retired member of the R.U.C who had taken up the civilian post of Office Manager in the C.I.D. office in Newry. He had been shot and injured on a previous occasion by the I.R.A. while serving in the Forkhill area. As he was being driven home by his wife, they were ambushed by terrorists and he was shot at as he sat in the car. He was then pulled out and repeatedly shot until he was dead as he lay on the ground in front of his wife. Mrs White, despite being distraught, ran to her husband and pulled out his personal protection weapon but was unable to use it against the murderers. Eamon Collins again had a part in targeting Albert White and in helping the murderers afterwards. In his book, 'Killing Rage' in which he explains how he helped in targeting Albert White and names the person who shot him. I with other police attended Albert's funeral at St Mary's Chapel in Newry which was yet another sad occasion.

In September, 1982, the World Angling Championships took place at Newry canal and police were very involved in traffic arrangements and in security at the venue. In general, the championships were a huge success without any major incidents and we kept a low key approach at the venue but had all the border crossing points well supervised with both police and military personnel. The Divisional Commander Keith Farlow took ill and was replaced by Bertie McCaffrey who acted up for a period. In early December, I had applied for promotion to

Superintendent and McCaffrey called me for interview and stated that he had been informed that there was friction between the Sub Divisional Commander, Billy Howard and I, and that he could not recommend me for promotion. I was surprised to hear this as I was unaware of any friction. I knew there had been friction between Billy Howard and Archie Hayes from previous encounters in the Community Relations Branch but I had not been involved. My immediate officers on that occasion certainly did me no favours. Notwithstanding, I was called to attend a promotion board.

Sergeant Eric Brown was in one of the District Mobile Support Units and very fond of accordion music. On occasions when I was playing at some of the parties which were organised in Newry when someone was leaving or at Christmas, he would sit beside me, really enjoying the music. On occasions he came to my house in Banbridge to hear me playing my electronic accordion. Constable Brian Quinn was also well known to me as he was the son of Inspector Tom Quinn whom I had served with both in Community Relations and in North Queen Street. I was on my way to Warrenpoint Station one day in January, when I heard over my police radio there had been a shooting at Rostrevor. I immediately drove there and an ambulance had just arrived. There were two unmarked police cars there and police were being taken into the ambulance. I found that they were Eric Brown, Brian Quinn and Percy Scott. It transpired that Brian and Eric were both dead and Percy had sustained grazes to the shoulder. Apparently, Percy who had been the driver of the police car, noticed what he thought was a suspicious car in Rostrevor. He got out of the police car and approached the other car before the other police were out of the car. A gunman jumped out and opened fire, firstly on him and then ran to the police car, shooting both policemen before they could alight. Percy exchanged fire with the gunman which later transpired he had injured the driver of the suspect vehicle in the foot.

I immediately organised Vehicle Check Points throughout and

asked for additional D.M.S.U's to help with searches. C.I.D. began enquiries at the scene with Inspector Brian McKinty in charge. Eighteen houses which were suspected of helping the Provisionals were searched and the U.D.R was also tasked to set up V.C.P,s and search the area. The car involved was found pretty quickly in Warrenpoint and searches were concentrated in the immediate area. The Warrenpoint /Rostrevor/Hilltown area was sealed for a prolonged period but eventually additional police were required elsewhere. Again, Harry Walker and I had the unenviable task of calling at the homes of Eric Brown and speaking with his widow and at the home of Tom Quinn in Bangor to grieve the death of his son. I later attended both funerals. Eamon Collins in his book describes how he ferried the murderer and the guns from a safe house in Rostrevor to Dundalk later on that night when the V.C.P, had been lifted and how the driver of the car had been shot in the foot by the police returning fire. He also names the killer and driver and states the reason for being there was to assassinate an ex member of the U.D.R. a soft target , expected at the post office that morning.

On a Sunday morning in February, 1983, Reserve Constable Eddie Magill walked across from Warrenpoint Police Station to the grocery shop in the square to get his Sunday papers. He was ambushed by terrorists who fired a number of shots and was fatally injured before he could get back to the station. A hand grenade was thrown at the station by the terrorists as they made they escape and police in the sanger were unable to return fire as it was difficult to pinpoint the firing point. The following evening, I called with his parents in Glencairn, and again experienced a very sad house where it was impossible to put into words my feelings for the parents' loss. I remember contemplating at the time what it would be like to kill someone in cold blood and whether I could in fact do it if the occasion arose, but because of the killings and heartache I had been experiencing in the past couple of years, I felt that given the evidence and the opportunity, I would have had no difficulty in taking the lives of those who had murdered so many of my friends. Thankfully, the occasion never arose but at that time, I felt that I was capable.

The following day, Sergeant Gordon Wilson was killed in Armagh by an I.R.A. bomb on 21st February 1983 and because he was originally from Warrenpoint and a member of Warrenpoint Presbyterian Church, I was again closely involved with the funeral arrangements. The bomb which killed him was operated by remote control and it was only shortly into March 1983 when Fred Morton, a police reservist serving at Bessbrook Station, while driving his bread van, was shot to death as he began his bread round on the Tandragee Road not far from his house. His three killers used a car to drive along side him and open up with automatic weapons. Again a soft target, Fred was killed instantly and his van careered into the left side of the road ending up on its side. It was suspected the killers were a unit operating from Dundalk who had a few safe houses in the Newry area where they lay up until the road blocks had been taken off, then returned to Dundalk. This was the reason that I was continually asking for army check points to be kept south of Newry. I was at the follow up of the scene of this murder and also attended Fred's funeral.

On 6th May, 1983, after finishing duty at 5.30pm, I was recalled to duty at 7.30pm by a report that a body was lying at the border at Clontigora. I requested an army fly over scene but was refused. I requested an army cordon be set up but was refused. I then got in touch with the Irish Authorities and asked for Garda and Irish Army presence on the southern side of the border which were set up as requested. The next morning, I went with Superintendent Billy Smith, the border Superintendent, who had replaced the late Stanley Hanna, to the scene. We found there was indeed a body wrapped in black polystyrene which turned out to be that of Eric Dale, a purported I.N.L.A. member which bore all the indications of an execution. He had been shot in the back of the head and covered in a bin bag. Later intelligence suggested that he was killed by members of the I.N.L.A who suspected he was a police informer. On the same date, there were bombs in Rostrevor and mortars fired at Crossmaglen Station.

In June, the same year, a call was received to a bomb being planted at Vision Hire, Margaret Street. I attended the scene with other police and we came under automatic fire from North Street Flats. D/Const Trevor Boyce was injured and D/Const John Horan received a graze to his side. Sergeant Stubber returned fire with his hand gun and I requested two units of military to North Street Flats to help to prevent further gunfire and to assist to establish firing point. Inspector McKeen was directed to take charge of I.C.P at Hill Street and Inspector Boyd directed to locate firing point at North Street flats. This was done and necessary agencies directed to same. Later I called at Daisyhill Hospital to see the injured member who fortunately was not seriously injured. The report of a bomb was a deliberate hoax to set up police for murder. On 30th June, an unsuccessful mortar attack took place on Newry Station. The station was evacuated as were some of the houses in Caulfield Place, beside the station and the Army Bomb Disposal Unit dealt with the mortars. There were no injuries on that occasion.

The Anniversary of internment in August was usually an excuse for causing civil unrest and 1983 was no exception. A number of cars were hi-jacked and burned and there was sporadic rioting resulting in police being required to fire F.R.G. (federal riot gun) rounds to disperse the rioters. A number of rioters were arrested including three from Londonderry who were taken to Armagh for questioning. On the protestant side, band parades were organised which required to be closely supervised. In September, three Detective Constables were making inquiries at St Joseph's School on the Armagh Road when there were fired on supposedly by the I.N.L.A. Their car was hit but they escaped injury. This was a wanton act of terrorism as many children were in danger of being injured. In the same month, six explosive devices were left at Fisher's timber yard causing a major fire which required six fire appliances to bring it under control. Army Bomb Disposal also attended the scene.

Newry ceased to be a Divisional Headquarter Station on 3rd of October, 1983. The office was moved to Armagh while Newry remained a Sub Division. On that date, bombs were placed at Campbell,s Garage in Rostrevor and at Sands factory at Basin walk. Bomb hoaxes also took place at Fisher's yard and Haldane & Shields. On 10th October, I, with the new Divisional Commander from Armagh, Leslie Hodgett, attended the scene of a fatal shooting at Hughes bookmaker's at Monaghan Street. John Henry McShane, a catholic, had been in the shop making a bet when gunmen raced in, approached him directly and shot him at point blank range. All the necessary agencies were tasked and searches organised throughout the sub division. It transpired that this was a case of mistaken identity as the gunmen though they were killing an R.U.C. detective who used the bookmakers. The late Eamon Collins was also involved in the targeting in this case. On

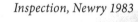

Inspection, Newry 1983

the same day there was an attempted bank robbery at the Allied Irish Bank in Hill Street but the terrorists left empty handed.

Constables Edmundson and Kennedy were driving an unmarked police car at Ballymoyer on 31st October. There was a car and trailer ahead of them of which they were suspicious and they stopped some way behind it. The back door of the trailer was lowered and they were suddenly subjected to heavy automatic gunfire from the back of the trailer. This was a carbon copy of the shooting of the three soldiers at Crossmaglen. Both constables managed to scramble out of their vehicle and use it for cover to return fire with their personal issue weapons. However they were both injured in the hail of bullets before the car and trailer drove off as it appeared the heavy duty weapon being used jammed. I Called at Daisyhill Hospital to see both Constables and spoke to their relatives. Fortunately, they both made a good recovery. I had known Nigel's father Victor who was a good friend of my brothers Harry and Wallace. Victor had asked me to phone him if anything happened to Nigel. I did this and was able to reassure him that Nigel's injuries were not life threatening and it was hoped he would make a full recovery.

We were not long into the new year before the murderers struck again. On 10th January, 1984, Reserve Constable Billy Fullerton was driving from work at Warrenpoint when he was ambushed at the Warrenpoint Road roundabout and shot to death. It appears that the terrorists drove along side when he slowed for the roundabout and opened fire, killing him through the driver's side window. I went to the scene of the shooting with the Deputy Divisional Commander Archie Hays and arranged vehicle check points and searches in the immediate area. The car involved was later recovered with spent cartridge cases inside. Mrs Fullerton collapsed and had to be taken to hospital when she heard her husband had been shot. I attended his funeral with other police on 13th January. The next brutal murders occurred on 31st January. I was on my way to Forkhill station when a got a call on my police radio that there had been an explosion on the Newry/ Forkhill Road. Within a couple of minutes I arrived at a scene of complete devastation. Inspector Henry Irvine was already there and had found the body of Sergeant Savage. We both searched over the hedge and found Constable Bingham's body completely decapitated. The unmarked police car being used by Sergeant Savage and Constable Bingham from Forkhill Station was completely disintegrated by the large explosion. I again had the unenviable task of notifying families of the deaths and attending both funerals of these two young men.

In February, grill bombs were placed on several shops in Hill Street in Newry and extensive damage was caused to all premises between Kildare Street and Margaret Square. A bomb also caused severe damage to Campbell's garage in Rostrevor. On 1st March, 84, I received a telephone call from headquarters which surprised me greatly. I had attended a promotion board but was not expecting anything because of the previous comments by my superior that I could not be recommended for promotion. I was told that I was to be promoted to Superintendent and to take up an appointment as Border Superintendent with effect from 9th March, operating from Armagh and replacing Billy Smith who had been transferred to other duties. I was delighted and began to make arrangements to obtain new uniforms and to clear my office prior to moving to Armagh. The station personnel held a function for me and I was presented with a silver tankard, suitably inscribed to mark my promotion and transfer. I was sorry to leave Newry as I was probably the longest serving officer there, having served from 1.9.78 until 9.3.84. I would be leaving many of the close friends who lost comrades and served through miserable years but who had still remained optimistic and cheerful. I consoled myself however that I would still be very much in touch as the border area included much of the Newry sub division.

Chapter 9
(Armagh)

I travelled to Armagh on the appointed day and settled into an office on the first floor. This was very different to the hustle and bustle of Newry Station to which I was accustomed. It was much quieter and my role changed considerably from that of being very much involved with duty arrangements and all that was happening in the station and sub-division, to one small quiet office in a long corridor. The Armagh Sub Divisional administration office was across the corridor so I made myself known to the staff, Constable Raymond Faulker and the girls. Whenever I left the station, I always informed Raymond as to my destination. My duties included getting to know the supervisory personnel in all of the border stations, both north and south of the border and introducing them to each other. There was already good communication between stations like Middletown and Monaghan and Newtownhamilton and Carrickmacross Newry and Dundalk. I endeavoured to have the good relationship between R.U.C. and Gardai improved and strengthened and often travelled to Monaghan, via Keady and Middleton to meet with my opposite number, Superintendent Tom Curran of the Garda. There were occasions when we met half way, this was usually at Long Nancy's, a public house half was between Monaghan and Armagh or in Caledon. I also visited Carrickmacross, Drumadd, Dundalk and Hackballscross to meet the Sergeants and Inspectors in those stations. It was useful to know intimately who was at the other end of the telephone when asking for cover on the Southern side of the border when setting up V.C.P's for clearance operations.

My duties also included arranging escorts and over-seeing explosives being transported from the South to the North. This was usually done by helicopter so there was a lot of flying time involved. Liaison with the Garda was paramount and a lot of time was taken up in pursuing this. I also performed foot patrols with personnel from Crossmaglen and Forkhill Stations on our side of the border to help my knowledge and maintain some contact with the local population. On occasions, I was required to perform duties as duty officer in the Division which included Newry and Armagh and this kept me in touch with all that was going on. I got to know the personnel in the Armagh sub division such as Keady, Tynan, Middletown and Markethill. Sergeant John Templeton who was Station Sergeant in Markethill for many years still lives in the area and we meet regularly at I.P.A. Golf Outings and discuss old times.

Meetings between Border Superintendents took place in Dublin, Armagh and Londonderry on a frequent basis and I attended these meetings with Chief Superintendent Robin Sinclair from Headquarters. I was also required to go to England to lecture incoming troops such as the parachute regiment or marines before they embarked in South Armagh for their four month tour. It was necessary to explain the need to refrain from alienating the bulk of the population in South Armagh by heavy handedness at road stops etc. Sergeant Cyril Simpson acted as liaison officer between the police and army at Bessbrook Mill and I used his expertise and knowledge of the South Armagh area and he accompanied me in many visits to border stations, North and South.

It was not long before the I.R.A struck again by way of a huge explosion against a police vehicle on the Crossmaglen Road at Camlough. On 18th May, 1984, Constables Mark Elwood, Trevor Elliott and Neville Gray were driving along the Crossmaglen Road towards Camlough Road when a huge culvert bomb was set off below their vehicle. Trevor was killed instantly and I visited the scene immediately afterwards and found Neville and Mark had been taken to hospital where Neville died the next day from his wounds. Mark eventually recovered from his injuries but was severely disabled. I had known Trevor Elliott particularly well as he was an excellent carpenter and had fitted a floor to my roof space in Banbridge, only a month previously. He was not only a good policeman but a wonderful husband and father and I again had the unenviable task of going to his home at Tandragee with A.C.C. Blair Wallace, Superintendents Brian Lally and Archie Hays to tell his wife that her husband was dead. When she opened the door and looked at our faces, she just fell into my arms with grief. These are moments I will never forget. I attended both funerals at Tandragee and Dromara together with other police from the Division.

On 29th May, an army patrol was ambushed by an explosive device at Crossmaglen. One soldier was killed and another injured. I went immediately by helicopter to the scene and liased with Garda to provide cover on the Southern side of the border while a clearance operation was underway. The injured soldier was removed immediately to Musgrave Park Hospital by helicopter. In early June, a lorry had been hi-jacked and an unsuccessful attempt made to mortar bomb Forkhill Station. The Gardai later found the lorry set up with home made mortars.

I had come to know Mr Eugene Connolly who was a member of the new police authority and lived in Keady. I very much admired this man who lived in such a difficult area in South Armagh, yet still believed in supporting law and order despite being constantly under threat. Eugene needed a heart replacement but expressed to me his wish to travel by helicopter to Crossmaglen and meet the station personnel and felt he was up to it. I arranged a trip and on 7th August, we flew to Crossmaglen and Eugene met the station party and Inspector Bob Green. He was delighted with his trip but unfortunately his health deteriorated soon after this and he passed away before a replacement heart could be found. A great loss to all that was decent in the Keady area.

On 19th October, 1984, terrorists hi-jacked a petrol tanker south of Crossmaglen. I went with D/const Derek Bradley and D/Const Mervyn Gibson, scenes of crime officers, to the scene. A bomb had been placed convenient to the tanker and was found by the army explosive team. It was blown up by a controlled explosion and we were anxious to pick up the remnants of the devices for forensic examination and get a helicopter flight out before dark. We asked permission from the Army Explosive Officer at the scene and he told us to go ahead. We gathered up as much of the device as we needed and had just moved away about fifty yards when suddenly there was a huge explosion and the spot we were standing on disintegrated, throwing debris about sixty feet in the air. We had been standing on top of a secondary explosive device of about 500 lbs timed to kill anyone who had found the first bomb. Again, it demonstrated the lengths these murderers were prepared to go to kill police and soldiers and we thanked our lucky stars that we had missed death by a few feet.

Early in November, when I acting duty officer at Newry, Operations Room received a call to a burglary at Glenhill Park. A mobile patrol of two Constables were dispatched to the house but when they went to the door there was no answer. I informed them by radio telephone to leave the area immediately. We later found that two families had been taken hostage in the cul-de sac. The first family taken hostage lived in the second house from the end of the street on the left. The second family lived facing down the street where there was a clear view of all houses. Both families were held in this house. Apparently, a bomb had been set inside the front door of the first hostages' house which was to be triggered from the second hostages' house by means of a command wire which had been passed along the back of the houses. It transpired that the person living in the end house on the left went out to his rear yard and not knowing what was happening, saw two wires running across his back yard. Thinking it was children' pranks, he cut the wires and threw them in his bin. This action obviously saved the lives of the two Constables who must have approached the door shortly afterwards. We could easily have had two more casualties but luck was on our side on this occasion.

A good friend of mine, Sergeant Frank Murphy, working with the Community Relations Branch in Armagh was driving an unmarked police minibus from Drumsallen Primary School were he had just dropped off children competing in an inter school quiz competition. When he was passing out of the school gates, terrorist gunmen opened fire at point blank range from a parked vehicle and he was killed instantly. Some of the bullets which had been fired from three separate weapons actually struck the school building where the children were watching. Again, another extremely sad occasion when I attended Frank's funeral at Banbridge with a number of his police comrades.

I received information from Special Branch that I was being specifically targeted by senior members of the I.R.A as a high profile target in Newry and I was aware I had been followed on more that one occasion in my car. At this time, I was afraid that they might follow me to my home address so I made a point of never using the same route and back-tracking between the station and my home. I also used different cars but the information was so strong that it was suggested that I use the S.P.E.D. scheme and move house. Marie and I began to look for a house and one Sunday, while driving along the Derryboy Road, we noticed a bungalow with a 'for sale' sign which had fallen down. We stopped and went to the door to find out if the house was still on the market. It transpired that I knew the people David and Janette Dickson so we were invited in. We were shown around and liked the house and gardens so we decided to make Davy an offer which he accepted. It was a long way to travel to work but at least the family would be safe. It also meant a complete disruption for family as Gary had just passed the 11 plus examination and was expected to go to Banbridge Acadamy. However, I arranged for him to spend a few weeks at Derryboye Primary before moving to Down High School at Downpatrick. This was useful as he made friends who would be travelling with him to the Grammar School.

I was travelling home on 28th February, 1985 when I heard a

H Squad Medal Presentation 1985

call over the police radio that Newry Station had been attacked by mortars and there were fatalities. I turned the car in the road and returned to Newry after phoning Marie and telling her that I was alright. There was a scene of complete devastation. The temporary building which had been a canteen in the yard had taken a direct hit and nine police had been killed with another thirty police and civilians injured. Inspector Errol McDowell was sitting with Chief Inspector Alex Donaldson in the canteen when he heard the thud of the first mortars which fell short. He immediately yelled mortars and raced to the door when the third mortar struck the canteen. He was blown outside but the others did not get out in time. He was lucky to be alive and his quick reflexes saved his life. Alex Donaldson was killed. I assisted with the clearance operation and arranged to have families of the deceased informed. Body parts were being picked up all over the yard and even the next day when members of Newry Council were expressing their condolences in the Divisional commander's office on the top floor, we found a hand lying on the outside window sill which had been missed in the clear up.

Everyone in Newry was shocked at this ferocious attack and the nuns from the convent in Catherine Street came down to offer their help and sympathy. The Chief Constable, Sir John Hermon, arrived the next day and I informed him that the nuns had been very helpful and perhaps he should pay them a visit and thank them for their concern. He did as I suggested and was well received at the convent. The funeral arrangements then began to take place and many of the Gardai officers came along to show their support. I went with Chief Superintendent Mike Bohan from Drogheda and Superintendent Harry Walker to Chief Inspector Alex Donaldson's funeral at Kilkeel. This atrocity was followed by another on 20th May, 1985. Inspector Billy Wilson had just arrived at Newry and was anxious to find out the boundaries of the Newry Sub-Division and the border with the Irish Republic. He went to the border with three other police in an armour plated police car to escort a security vehicle coming from the South. As they passed a trailer parked on their left, a huge explosion in the region of 1000lbs was detonated and the car was completely demolished, killing all four police inside, Inspector Billy Wilson, the driver W/con Tracy Doak, Constable David Baird and R/Constable Stephen Rodgers.

In June a drive - by shooting took place at the police sub-station at Downshire Road Newry when R/Const D Russell was injured while leaving the station. Fortunately, it was not fatal, but was a timely reminder of the need for utmost vigilance by all personnel when entering or leaving the stations. A mortar attack took place at Crossmaglen station in the month of June. I went immediately to Crossmaglen by helicopter and found none of the station party had been injured and no casualties. In the same month, Garda Sergeant Pat Morrissy was murdered south of the border and I requested army helicopter at Bessbrook to take to the air to help with search for fugitives. I attended Sergeant Morrissy's funeral at

Drogheda with Superintendent Lally and Chief Superintendent Mick Bohan. The pressure of work in the Armagh/Newry area at this time was never ending as the personnel had not only the ordinary policing duties to contend with but also the never-ending threat of terrorist attack. Each individual had their own way of dealing with the situation and on occasions, too many of us probably resorted to relaxing through intake of liquor. We had parties on special occasions for those leaving or transferred and I would bring out the piano accordion and entertain by way of a sing - song. This was our way of relieving the pressure.

Marie and I were beginning to enjoy the countryside at our new house in Derryboye. I bought a tourer caravan and always tried to get annual leave leading up to the British Golf Championships. We toured to whatever venue the championships were held during their practice week and our son Gary also enjoyed watching the golfers and walking around with the golfing greats as they practised before the tournament. We had the privilege of having a pee with Jack Nicholas in a make shift toilet at Turnberry. We found him a pleasant person with no airs or graces and very easy to converse with. We bought Gary a grass track motor cycle and although he was only twelve years old, he became very proficient at racing the motor cycle around the three acre field behind our house. I hoped this would get the notion for motor cycles and speed out of his system before he was the age for a licence. I also had a twenty bore and twelve bore shotgun and we enjoyed some of Gary's teenage years hunting for rabbits and pigeons in the adjoining fields and bogs. The time I spent with my son made me realise how much I had missed the childhood of my three daughters through pressure of police work. Gary wanted a pup so we got a black Labrador which we named Clint. He was a great dog and gave us much love and pleasure at Derryboye.

During the marching season, there were many confrontations at Portadown, the heart of Loyalism where there was opposition to orange parades through a Catholic area. There were almost fifteen hundred loyalist marches and around four-hundred republican marches. Although there were only about fifty contentious parades, the cost of policing them was astronomical. The trouble started at Garvaghy Road where police were made to confront marching loyalists. I performed duty at Garvaghy Road and it became clear to me that there is very little difference between a Catholic thug and a Protestant thug when they confront the police. We were now in direct conflict with the protestant majority population and indeed following the confrontations, members of the R.U.C. living in protestant areas had petrol bombs hurled at their homes by so called loyalists and many had to leave in a hurry. Irresponsible unionist politicians stoked the high feelings against the police by suggesting that the R.U.C. was following a 'Dublin agenda', and there were all sorts of rumours flying about changes in uniform etc.

The Anglo Irish agreement was signed by Margaret Thatcher and Garret Fitzgerald in November, 1985 after some pressure on Thatcher from the United States and there followed weeks of protestant unrest and conflict. I was in charge of a party of police in Keady, a mainly Catholic town, where about two hundred protestants, which on that occasion can only be described as rabble, assembled with the intention of having a protest march through the town. It was led by a D.U.P. Councillor who was agitating the crowd and giving the police dog's abuse. He continually stuck his ugly mug close up to my face and shouted and sneered, "Who elected you – Who elected you". I was tempted to see if my blackthorn stick would fit in his nostril but held my peace. They were stopped from marching after much pushing and shoving so it was worth the abuse to see them eventually leave the town without their march. It saddens me that some of the same so called 'law abiding citizens' or low life now hold office in Government.

On the day the Anglo-Irish agreement was signed, 15th November, 1985, I received a call that two constables had been injured by an explosion while on patrol on Castleblaney Road. I attended the scene and learned that Constable David Hanson had been killed and Constable Mark Wright injured. I went to Crossmaglen Station and arranged to have David's girl-friend call at Donegall Pass Station. Later that evening, I visited David's home at Lisburn and spoke to his parents and brother. I then later arranged through Grosvenor Road police to visit Constable Mark Wright in the Royal Victoria Hospital on the same day as I attended David's funeral.

Shortly after this in December, Tynan station was attacked by mortars and almost completely demolished by fire. Four Police officers were injured and on arrival at the scene I found that three mortars had exploded and one left unexploded. I liased with the border superintendent in Monaghan and arranged a follow –up search on the southern side of the border. Some weapons were found by the Gardai during the follow – up. On 21st December, I attended the home of Det/Const Billy Galbraith who had died as the result of a shooting incident. I informed the Divisional Commander, Billy Stewart, and arranged for the Chief Constable to visit the home.

In January, 1986, I was notified to attend an Intermediate Command Course at Bramshill College in Hampshire. The object of this three month course was to prepare selected officers of Superintendent rank to undertake the additional responsibilities involved in Divisional or Departmental Command. Having been selected for this course, I felt that I was being prepared for a Divisional Command somewhere in the province and I was going to give it my best shot. There were thirty one other officers there from Constabularies from all over England from the Metropolitian to Merseyside. I made many friends and four in particular were Chief Superintendent George Columbo from Gibralter, Superintendent Dave Coggan from Avon and Somerset, Superintendent Barrie Jeffrey from Humberside and Detective Superintendent Barry Stewart from Northumbria. George like me did not get home at week-ends so we spent time together, tasting the local food and sampling the local ale. We once went to London and attended an Opera at the West End. I was later to visit George at Gibralter when on holidays in Spain and he and his good wife gave Marie and I a great reception. At the time there had been some hostage situations and one of the role play scenarios at the college was to be in charge of a situation where hostages had been seized and decisions required to be made as to when the police would hand over to the military authorities, thereby relinquishing control over the situation. My previous experiences in working with military probably stood me in good stead and I feel I performed well in these role play situations.

A number of us also went to Muchengladbach in Germany to study control of football matches and how the German police dealt with football hooligans. The Metropolitian Officers were generally well versed in these situations and I gathered a lot of useful information. The local police in Germany used cameras and policed the crowds by dividing the terraces into sectors with small groups of easily identifiable officers in coloured coats and radio receiver headgear in each sector. The camera team then directed the officers to potential trouble makers. I was of the opinion that Football Clubs should either be made to pay for policing at matches or else police the matches with their own stewards. The command course was very interesting and useful and on arriving home after three months, I found I had been given a very good report. I also received notification I had been transferred to Belfast as Deputy Head of the Community Relations Branch at Lisnasharragh.

I had mixed feelings about the transfer. I was very sorry to leave all my friends in Newry and Armagh were I had served for almost eight years. These people had policed under the most terrifying conditions, yet still retained their sense of purpose and sense of humour and I knew I would miss them. On the other hand, my return journey to work daily was in the region of one hundred miles which put an extra two hours on my working day. The transfer would mean a lot less travelling to work and more time at home.

Chapter 10
(Community Relations 2)

I gathered up my belongings and attended a function held in my honour and said my goodbyes. The following day, 21st March, 1986, I arrived in Lisnasharragh and met the head of the Community Relations Branch, Chief Superintendent Ernie Bleakney. My office was opposite his and I began to get accustomed to a new but none the less demanding way of life. The next few months were spent in finding out everything that the Community Relations and Juvenile Liaison staff was involved with in each sub division. This included supervising summer camps with children from different religious and ethnic backgrounds, arranging top of the form competitions in schools, running blue lamp discos, arranging five a side football and boxing competitions. It also entailed visiting every Divisional and Sub -divisional commander and endeavouring to promote the ideals of community relations throughout the province and supervision of and help and encouragement to all Community relations staff. It was also necessary to meet and know those bodies involved with youth work and persons in Government Departments involved in improving relationships. I was also required to lecture at any courses held for Inspectors. I acted on occasions as an Inspecting officer at passing out parades for Royal Ulster Constabulary Reserves. While the duties were quite different from those as a border Superintendent, they were demanding.

I had been elected to the position of Captain in the Royal Ulster Constabulary Golfing Society and in 1986, the British Championships were to be played at Portrush. I had found that competitive golf and spending quality time with my family were the only two things that took my mind away from my job. As Captain, I was heavily involved in the arrangements for the championships

Lecture to Reserves 1985

and was given sports leave. When the three day event began, the R.U.C. team performed quite well. The performance of Constable Bobby Wallace in the individual competition was out-standing. It was a cold blustery day at Portrush and Bobby was playing well and amongst the leaders. He got a good par at the dangerous fourteenth 'Calamity' hole and hit a good drive against the wind at the next hole, the fifteenth, known as 'Purgatory'. However, his approach shot to the green caught the right hand bunker and he played a poor bunker shot which landed precariously on the sloped grass side of the bunker. The wind was blowing hard and Bobby walked backwards and forwards along the length of a forty foot putt line weighing up the 'borrows' on the putt. I was praying he would hurry up and take the putt before the wind blew it back in the bunker. Eventually, he bent over the putt and after what seemed like an age, he struck it firmly. The ball rolled and rolled and eventually dropped into the hole. Bobby went on to win and become British Police Champion and it was a proud moment when I presented him with his winner's prize.

Other headquarter staff in Community Relations were Chief Inspector Jimmy Nairn, Inspector Ross Penny and Inspector Dennis Quinn. We became a close knit unit, working very well with each other. Duties on a daily basis were mainly of a supervisory nature and entailed travelling and visiting C.R. Staff and Divisional and Sub Divisional Commanders throughout Northern Ireland. The Branch also rented a remote cottage between Ballymena and Carnlough at a place called Longmore where children and youth clubs from both religions were taken for short periods at a time so they could relate to each other and the police. Another useful venue for meetings was at Corrymeela, near Ballycastle where numerous seminars were attended. Even those close to paramilitary organisations met together and discussed their problems with a view to co-operating in a peaceful way.

When involved with the intermediate command course at Bramshill, I noticed that many of the Superintendents were graduates and obtained financial help from their respective forces in furthering their education and studying in their own time. I applied for help in 1986 and began a course of study in social sciences with the Open University which would hopefully lead to a B.A. Degree. My previous education results within the R.U.C. and attendance at the Intermediate command course were taken into consideration with my application and I was accepted as a student. My studies in my own time were conducted through attending classes at Newtownards technical college each week and also attending a tutor who set assignments on a monthly basis. C.R. duties continued unabated and lectures on Community Relations were introduced into probationer training at Garnerville. Lectures on the workings of the branch were also given to foreign dignitaries at Headquarters and there were continued demands in dealing with outward bound schemes and rambles and prize presentations organised by the branch throughout the summer. In

November, 1986, the Chief Constable's wife, Lady Hermon, died. I attended her funeral as she was a real lady for whom I had great respect, although I admit I did not feel the same for Sir John.

Community Relations duties were beginning to become routine and while terrorism continued, there were never many signs of real progress to encourage those working so diligently. Difficulties still persisted in hard areas, both Protestant and Catholic and C.R. staff often felt they were working in a vacuum, both in trying to convince their colleagues and the warring factions that it was the best way forward. I was still involved with the R.U.C. Golfing society and was appointed non-playing Captain of the R.U.C. Police Team to play in the British Championships at Meon Valley Golf Course in Hampshire. I was having a round of golf with Jamie Flanagan, the former chief constable, when I took a severe pain in the chest. I knew it was heart trouble but I was playing so well, I didn't feel like stopping. However, I decided to stop after nine holes and went to the hotel and lay down for a couple of hours. The pain

R.U.C. Golf Team 1987.

subsided and I was able to continue with the evening meal. The police team did very well in that championship, winning both the Looms Trophy and International Shield.

The following week-end, when I returned home, I had a four ball match to play at my own golf club at Mahee. My partner, Billy McClements and I were playing against the brothers, Robert and Jim McClenaghan. I took a pain in my chest at the second hole which continued throughout the match. Billy actually had to pull my trolly up the hills. The match went to the nineteenth hole and by this time, the pain had worsened so I decided I would go to my doctor the next morning. This I did and was sent immediately for an angio-gram to the Royal Victoria Hospital. The surgeon, Mr Jack Cleland, told me I had four blockages to the coronary arteries. I should go home and do nothing and he would operate in three weeks. He was as good as his word and I was given a quadruple by-pass operation on 23rd July, 1987, my daughter Valerie's thirty-second birthday. I was off work for some time and began to build up my health by walking between telegraph poles and increasing the number each week.

It was six months before I was able to resume duties at Headquarters but it was quite easy to slip into the routine and before long I was back in harness. My boss Ernie Bleakney had been replaced in my absence by Chief Superintendent Emily Barnett and the branch continued to operate in much the same way. In May, 1988, I was given duty credits to attend a week's summer school at U.M.I.S.T. University in Manchester in connection with my studies. Chief Superintendent John Hamilton was on the same course so I had some company. The remainder of the summer was taken up by supervision duties, attending selection boards for the R.U.C. and C.R. Branch, attending camps at Longmore, Boxing competitions at Newtownards, ramble presentations, top of the form competitions ,blue lamp discos and meetings with Government, Housing Executive, Y.M.C.A., Social Services, Education and Probation and other bodies throughout the province. In October, I attended an examination at Stranmillis College for the first part of my degree course and was successful in obtaining a good pass.

Golf at Mahee was still very much on the agenda and club competitions were held every week-end. Both the Ulster Cup team and the Junior Cup teams were competing well and a team comprising of players from both these teams was selected for the Jimmy Bruen Foursomes, an all-Ireland competition. I was part of the 1988 team which did exceptionally well in winning the Ulster Championship by defeating the favourites, Warrenpoint, at Belvoir, and then went on to Little Island to compete in the All-Ireland semi-final. Unfortunately, we were defeated in the semi-final by a strong team from Clonmel who went on to win the All Ireland title that year.

Mahee Island G.C. Ulster Champions 1989

On 20th March, 1989, an event occured which saddened me greatly and took my mind back from the relative hum-drum and safety of police Headquarters, to the sharp end of policing in South Armagh. Chief Superintendent Harry Breen and Superintendent Bob Buchanan had been to Dundalk to meet with their Gardai counterparts, a journey I had made on many occasions. Both were close friends of mine, Harry having served with me in Newry and Bob replaced me as Border Superintendent. I believe that Bob was about to be transferred to Newtownards after his service on the border and he went to Dundalk to say his farewells to his Gardai counterparts. When they left the station, they returned via Jonesboro and ran into an I.R.A ambush where they were attacked by heavy machine gun fire. Bob was killed instantly and Harry was killed as he tried to leave the vehicle. Both men were unarmed and this callous act was again carried out by I.R.A. murderers and thugs. It was suspected at the time they had been set up by an informer but the meeting had been arranged at short notice and their route could not have been known to anyone. I had travelled many times to a number of stations in border area of the South. I often drove deeper into the South before returning and again often doubled back on my route. I also advised Bob when he took over from me that he should vary his route between home and station and also when he was travelling between his station and Southern Ireland. I suggested his movements be on a need to know basis, not to every Tom Dick or Harry who might demand to know them. It would appear that the murderers followed them into Dundalk and then used a car and radio transmitter to follow them home and set up the ambush. I have my own suspicions as to the facts. At that time the I.R.A. was of such strength in South Armagh that they could have had two or more routes covered.

I attended both homes to offer condolences to their relatives, attended both funerals, then back to the usual Community Relations Duties. Sixth form seminars were arranged between Catholic and Protestant schools and help given to the organisers of the Milk Cup football competition held yearly in Coleraine where youth football teams from all over the world compete. I also gave a presentation on Community Relations to Chief Superintendents from a Senior Command Course at Bramshill college. In April 1990 another tragedy occurred near our home on the Derryboy Road. The Jackson family were farmers and good neighbours who lived close to us. Their little girl rode her pedal cycle from their yard onto the road and into the path of a car and was fatally injured. Marie and I had walked this road regularly with our dog Clint, There was great sadness in the household and at the funeral in Raffrey. I realised that I had spent the past thirty years in dealing with problems created by other people and I had in fact missed my children growing up. My girls were all adults and I was so much involved in my work that I had missed much of their childhood. The death of the little girl made me realise there was more to life than constant pressure from policing.

I decided I was not getting sufficient job satisfaction from Community Relations. I was happier in an ordinary police duty scenario but because of my health problems, it was unlikely that I would be given a Divisional Command so I began to contemplate retirement. I felt I would need to do something to occupy my time and was still very much involved with my golf club. I spoke to Eric Trevorrow, who was acting Honorary Secretary but had indicated he was about to retire so I applied for the post and was accepted in 1989. This was an unpaid position but it would give me sufficient interest in something I enjoyed. I had served for twenty-nine years and was very proud of my service, associated with one of the finest police forces in the world. I found that I could retire on medical grounds with a full pension so I decided to end my service with the Royal Ulster Constabulary on 18th May, 1991. A function was held in my honour at La Mon House Hotel and I was delighted that senior officers including Deputy Chief Constable Michael McAtamney, Chief Superintendent Paddy McCullough and Chief Superintendent Emily Guy together with most of the Community

Relations Staff from all over the province, attended. I was given a beautiful oil-painting of a golfing scene with Mountains in the background as a parting gift from the Community Relations Branch.

Retirement, Guest of Honour 1991

Chapter 11
(Retirement)

I was now embarking on a complete change in life-style. No more worries about everyday policing matters, or about getting things done in time and I moved into a more relaxed frame of mind. Marie had looked after me and the children since we were married and I felt it was time to give something back. We made plans to spend most of our time together and to enjoy our holidays. I continued with my studies to obtain a degree at my own expense. My son Gary had applied to join the Royal Ulster Constabulary and he was accepted. A very proud father and mother attended his passing out parade at Garnerville Training Centre in September, the same year I had left the force.

Gary at Crossmaglen

Gary followed in my footsteps and went on transfer to Newry when he finished his training. He later volunteered to go to Crossmaglen where he served for three years through a very difficult and dangerous period and is still serving in Newtownards.

My energies were now directed towards my family and running the golf club. Mahee continued to compete well in the Jimmy Bruen Shield competition. In 1991, we defeated Clandeboye in the first round, Ballymena at Lurgan in the second round, Ballyclare at Carrickfergus in the third round. I particularly remember this match as my playing partner, Colin Wilson, and I were three down with four to play and at that stage the score was two matches each. We won the next three holes to level the match and Colin struck the final putt to win on the eighteenth green. We beat Rathmore at Knock in the Ulster final to become Ulster champions for the second time. We were scheduled to play the All Ireland semi finals against Dungarvan at Malone Golf Club and managed to beat them to meet Beechpark in the final. We also won the final and I was chuffed that my partners, Ricky Dodds, Colin Wilson

Mahee All Ireland Champions 1991

and I had gone through the tournament unbeaten and I now had an All Ireland 'gold' medal to add to my Ulster 'bronze'. The celebrations continued well into the night and we were later given a civic reception by Ards Borough Council for our achievements.

Retirement in the early nineteen nineties meant getting involved with and enjoying our grand-children who came to our house in the country and stayed for a week at a time during the school holidays. It started with Natasha and Trudy, the older girls, then progressed to Carly, Jonathan and Kathy as they got older. I continued with my studies and extended my interests in golf by joining the Irish Association of Left Handed Golfers and the Northern Ireland Association of Secretary Managers, (N.I.S.M.A.) These interests kept me busy, not only in the business end of golf but also provided a lot of playing time which kept me reasonably fit. I also became secretary of N.I.S.M.A. when the late Joe Crozier of Carnalea Golf Club gave it up and remained secretary for four years. I received notification in 1992 that I had obtained a B.A. degree from the Open University and decided to continue study for an honours degree. I also enjoyed my music, having bought

Fred Daly Pro Am

an electronic organ, together with the electronic accordion. Marie and I continued to walk a couple of miles daily with our dog Clint so I had no difficulty in filling my time. I had the pleasure of playing as one of Mahee's representatives at the first Fred Daly Pro-Am golf tournament at Balmoral.

Marie and I decided to have a good holiday in the summer of 1994. The world cup of football was taking place in Orlando, Florida and the left hander's world amateur golf championships were being held at West Palm Beach, on the P.G.A's course. We decided to take our holidays in June to co-incide with these events. We also arranged to finish off with a short cruise to the Bahamas. The weather in Miami was beautiful when we arrived so we hired a car for the drive to West Palm Beach. Unfortunately, we lost our way in Miami and found ourselves in a sinister area where groups of young black teenagers were hanging about the street corners and as darkness was falling, we decided to try and get somewhere to stay for the night and so went to the first available rooms we could find. The accommodation was not of a high standard but the bed was clean and we were glad to be off the street. While lying in bed and discussing the days events, I felt something sharp on the front of my chest. I worked at it with my fingers and began to pull it out. It turned out to be a piece of stitching about four inches long which had been left in my chest since my bypass operation in 1987.

The next day we moved along the coast to Fort Lauderdale, then to West Palm Beach where we met up with the other members of the Irish Left Hander's Association including Jerry Bradley, the secretary of the Irish section and Kevin McVeigh and his wife Joan from Warrenpoint. We had a look around the P.G.A.complex where we were staying and the accommodation was luxurious compared with the previous night. After registration, we were informed we were playing in the open competition and I was interested to find my first round playing partners were Peter Read and Barry Huckstepp, both from Australia. After a practise round on the course, I began to realise how difficult it was and to appreciate how well professional golfers played the game. While the men were playing golf, arrangements were made to take the non-playing wives on a boat trip and then for a shopping spree at Rodeo Drive. Needless to say, there were a few anxious golfers waiting to find out whether they was still some cash left in their account after this bout of shopping. I was not on my game and found the course so different from what I was accustomed to. There was water everywhere and I found that it was not possible to bounce the ball on to the green from water.

After the first day's play, we were then placed into groups in which our golf was compatible. I ended up with two Americans, one who was slightly inebriated before we started to play and had a golf bag full of cans of beer which he duly lowered during the round. When we came to the feature hole of the course, the seventeenth, an island green requiring a carry of one hundred and eighty yards over water, he proceeded to put thirteen balls into the water all around the green. He borrowed two balls from me before giving it up as a hopeless task. By this time he could barely walk but was still able to purchase more beer from a mobile shop which followed him around the course. A great character who was 'only there for the beer'. After three very enjoyable days, Marie and I said our good-byes to the left-handers and moved on to Orlando .

We booked into a hotel in International Drive and began to make inquiries as to the possibility of getting tickets for the world cup match, Ireland v Mexico which was due to be played in a couple of days. A waiter at the hotel said he had a couple of tickets which he would sell for fifty dollars. I was delighted and almost broke his arm for the tickets. On the day, Marie and I set off for the match and we were very impressed with the traffic arrangements. We were taken to a particular site in the bus and given a particular colour wrist band. There were huge balloons about seventy feet in the air of different colours around the ground and we were told to head towards the colour of our wrist band. We then entered the ground with the minimum of fuss and when the match was concluded, the same arrangement applied, head towards the colour of your wrist band. There were over one hundred thousand people and the game was played in beautiful sunshine. Unfortunately, Ireland was beaten but we had a wonderful time. I was greatly impressed by the organisation at this game and there were no problems whatsoever in clearing the ground after the match.

Ireland v Mexico Orlando 1994.

We left Orlando and drove to Cape Canaveral on the east coast. Here we boarded the 'Big Red Boat' for a three day cruise to the Bahamas. The size of the ship impressed me and when we boarded, I found we had to take the lift to our cabin which was seven floors down. Luckily, the cabin window was still above the water line and before we knew it, we were about a mile off-shore.

Marie looked at the shore and then began to panic saying, 'Get me back. I can't go any further.' I'm afraid I was a bit short with her as I asked her could she swim as that was the only way she was getting back but she finally got a grip and settled down. We dressed for dinner and were seated with two lovely, rather timid people from Texas who admitted to us that when they heard we were from Belfast, they were terrified as they had heard all the bad publicity and their imagination had run riot. However, when they met us they were delighted that we were not terrorists and we had a quite enjoyable time together. The waiters and waitresses on the cruise put on a different show-time theme every night and the quality of the entertainment was excellent.

Big Red Boat 1994

An amusing incident occurred when we left the ship at Nassau to go to a night club for a show. We were picked up by a mini bus with a local black driver who was a bit of a character. In the Bahamas, they drive on the left side of the road, similar to the U.K. but the Americans on the bus did not know this. The driver was shouting and singing as he drove along and because he was driving on the left, the Americans on board thought he was drunk and were yelling that he was driving on the wrong side of the road. He took great pleasure in frightening the life out of them. We had a wonderful time on board the Big Red Boat, the food and entertainment were excellent although we both feel that three days cruising was just about right. The long flight home ended a very enjoyable holiday.

Meet the Captain

Our fortieth (Ruby) wedding Anniversary fell on 27th January, 1995. My son Gary and daughter Carol arranged to surprise us by having a family get together at Clandeboye Lodge Hotel. It was a wonderful evening with the family including my mother and the grandchildren. I was also elected Captain of Mahee Island Golf Club and while playing golf at an outing to City West Golf Club south of Dublin in March, I managed to hole out in one at the eleventh hole for my second hole in one. Captain's Day at Mahee in June went well and I was delighted that my son in law, Neil, won my Captain's prize, a Tyrone Crystal table lamp, particularly as my daughter Gwen had sent him out with strict instructions to win it. The highlight of my Captaincy at Mahee was when our juvenile section won the Sargaison Shield. The team was looked after by Stewart Warwick.

Sargaison Shield Winners 1995

In October, I also had the pleasure of obtaining my third 'hole in one' at an R.U.C. Golfing Society outing at the fourth hole at Royal County Down while playing with my son Gary, my friend Tommy Murphy and son in law Neil. By this stage I was playing a lot of golf and competed in the Irish Provincial Seniors competitions each year as I had managed to lower my golf handicap to eight.

A surprise awaited me towards the end of the year when my mother who was seventy six, informed me she was getting married to a widower, Tom Boyd, who lived in the fold. I was glad for her to have some company and they were married at a quiet ceremony at the Borough Council Offices in Newtownards in November.

We had by this time lived around twelve years at Derryboye and felt that a six bed-roomed house with over fifty windows to clean was a bit too much for us. The children were now all grown up and away and with three acres to look after which included a huge garden, we decided to look for something which would be easier to keep. We decided to move to a new house under construction at Beechfield, Bangor, and set plans in motion to sell. We were sorry to leave Derryboye but felt as we were getting on, it was the right thing to do. We sold and moved to Beechfield on the sixteenth of February, 1996 and moved into what was to be our home for the next six years. The left-handers World Championships were to be played at the Warwickshire in England in July, so our summer holidays were arranged around this. My grandmother, Georgena Bowman had taken ill in and passed away in the first week in September, aged ninety nine years. She had been a great character, an inspiration throughout my life and was also much loved by all our children. She was greatly missed. As Honorary Secretary of the Mahee Club and also of the Northern Ireland Secretary Manager's Association, my time for the rest of the year was taken up mostly by secretarial duties and playing golf with the left handers and various police societies of which I was still a member.

My fourball each Saturday morning at Mahee consisted of John Marshall (senior), John Marshall (junior), Davy Andrews and myself. John Marshall (senior) was an Irish Champion cross-country runner and Davy Andrews a champion motor cyclist and each in their own life time, would have a wonderful story to tell. They had been at Mahee as caddies since the club was formed and were excellent golfers and competitors. Unfortunately, Davy's wife died suddenly in January 1997 and we all attended the funeral at Maghermourne. In February, Marie and I enjoyed a two-week holiday in Lanzarote to get some winter sun. In September, each year, a club member, Mervyn Marshall, arranged a golfing week-end, generally in the South of |Ireland where about twenty members of Mahee would congregate and have an enjoyable week-end. This yearly outing still takes place to the present day.

Marie and I had arranged to go to Australia to co-incide with her sixtieth birthday in November and to take a three month break so we would have plenty of time to enjoy our holiday and to visit our daughter Valerie and her family and my brother Wallace. We headed off to London and from there to Singapore on Monday, 17th inst. On arrival at Singapore we were impressed by the cleanliness of the place, no chewing gum allowed, and enjoyed the very pleasant heat after the winter cold at home. We walked to Raffles Hotel and had the proverbial 'Gin Slinger' in the afternoon. We dined out at one of the quay side boat restaurants at Clarke's Quay on the Singapore river and cooked on a cone shaped pan, a delicious meal of chicken strips in herbs which were supplied by the restauranteur. The pleasant warm breeze and the city night lights reflecting from the river created a very special atmosphere for this meal and one to remember.

After a couple of days, we boarded a plane for Perth and arrived at Sullivan's hotel. The weather at Perth was still warm in the sun but noticeably cooler that Singapore. We booked a boat trip to Freemantle along the Swan river and were shown the house where Rolf Harris was supposed to have lived. I always take these alleged celebrity homes with a pinch of salt. We spoke to a girl from Magherafelt having recognised her Irish accent. It transpired she was competing in the world's triatholon Championship which was taking place in Freemantle. The world's Whitbread around the world yacht race was also taking place and the town was crowded. We had dinner in one of the Perth hotels when we returned. Later in the week we booked trips to a colonial house built by people named Stirling and to the Sandleford vineyard for some wine tasting. Met some people from Singapore, (head of operations of Singapore Airlines), and some interesting people from Japan and we decided to spend our last night in Perth by taking it easy. I was impressed by the free transport system in Perth where the red buses travelled north to south and the blue ones east to west. This meant parking was all arranged on the outskirts of the city and prevented congestion in the town.

We headed off early in the morning to catch a flight to Cairns which I had booked from home. On arrival at the airport in Perth, we were told that the particular flight had not been operating for at least six months. We began to panic but the operator suggested we get on a flight to Adelaide, then Brisbane then Cairns. As the flight was leaving shortly, we decided to take it and eventually arrived at Cairns with no extra costs. We booked into the Colonial Club and had an enjoyable meal of chicken and satay pork at the Homestead restaurant. It had been raining in Cairns for almost a fortnight before we arrived but the weather was warm and sunny during our stay. We hired a car for the drive to Sydney and drove north to Port Douglas, a beautiful sea-side resort near the Great Barrier Reef. We hired a boat trip to Green Island on the reef and

Green Island

spent a glorious day there, feeling like Robinson Crusoe, walking on the warm sand and swimming in the deep blue green sea. When we returned to the Colonial Club, we explored the whole complex and came across a beautiful white grand piano on which I could not resist having a tune. Marie took a photograph as I played the piano.

A week passed and we set off again along the Bruce Highway towards Townsville on the first part of our journey to Sydney. There were beautiful beaches along the route and we stopped off for a couple of days at places we found attractive. The highways were generally deserted and the temperature in places rose to forty degrees. I had been given a parcel by staff at our clinic in Bangor to give to Doctor Lavery who was practising in Townsville. We found his clinic easily enough and when he opened the parcel, it contained a bun and some chocolate which had melted in the extreme heat. Had I known what was in the parcel, I would have dumped it. We also stopped on the Bruce Highway and phoned Carol and Billy at home. It turned out that we had miscalculated the time and instead of it being ten o'clock in the evening, it was one o'clock in the morning. We apologised to Carol for this error but were informed that everything was fine at home. We drove to Ayr and then to Sarina Beach where we booked into a gorgeous suite right on the shore. The place was so lovely with palm trees, pool and a view overlooking a golden sandy beach, a sea green ocean and with a clear blue sky, we decided to stay for a few days. Unfortunately, I wrenched my elbow when stepping into a hole I did not see as it was filled with water. I grabbed a pole as I fell and tore some ligaments. This meant Marie had to drive for a while each day.

We then continued our journey passing through towns such as Gladstone, Caloundra, Brisbane, Ballina to Coff's Harbour, spending some time at each. The weather was great, sunny with good temperatures and it was all most enjoyable. We moved to Port Macquarie where my nephew Ian lived with his wife and children. Ian was the minister of a church in the town and we met some of his parishioners who were delighted to meet us and were high in their praise of the work Ian was doing in the parish. We called to meet them and spent some time with them before moving on towards 'The Entrance' and then Gosford and Sydney. On our way from Coff's Harbour to Port Macquarie, we came across road signs for Crossmaglen and Newry Island. I was certainly not expecting to see these and they took me back to my police service. It would appear that early pioneers from South Armagh must have settled there and brought their place names with them. Marie's neck began to be very painful probably because of all the driving and we decided she would have to see a doctor on arrival at Sydney.

We arrived at Valerie's house on Friday, 12th December, 1997, just about a week before Christmas. The weather was beautiful, about thirty degrees and it was hard to believe it was December. A friend of mine, Dawson Carrol and his wife Marie were holidaying at his house in Mona Vale and Marie and I called and spent enjoyable day with them at his local golf course followed by dinner in the evening. There had been a terrific hail storm a few days before and the hailstones as large as golf balls dented Dawson's car from top to bottom and actually smashed the rear window. Marie had her neck treated each week by the physiotherapist who looked after the Australian Cricket team and she began to get a bit of ease with it. We spent Christmas week with Val and family then travelled to the Hunter Valley with Wallace and Molly, sampling a few wines from Lindeman,s and other wineries. We also arranged to visit my son in law, Neil's, father Duncan in Melbourne, so we drove down through Canberra and met up with him and his wife, Robin. We stayed overnight with Duncan, then headed back to Sydney.

Our wedding anniversary was on the 27th January, so I arranged a meal for us at Centrepoint, a huge tower in central Sydney with a revolving restaurant which overlooked the city.

We went by train and had an enjoyable day exploring Sydney in beautiful sunshine, enjoyed the buskers in and around the harbour, followed by a wonderful meal in the tower restaurant at sunset. It was soon time to take our leave and we said our goodbyes to all the family at the beginning of February before boarding the plane to Los Angeles where we intended to spend the last week of our holiday. On arrival, the weather was atrocious and we were held at the airport by security for a considerable time while they checked our passports. I was getting a bit peeved with the dour security guards who didn't give any explanation as to why we were being detained. After about an hour, we were given back our passports and allowed to proceed without an explanation, a bad start. We booked into the Furama Hotel and decided we would take a minibus tour of the city which included Holywood, Bel Air Avenue, Sunset Strip, Saint Monica Beach and Fisherman's wharf. The rain was incessant so it was not what we expected. We were surprised by Sunset Strip where all the stars had their hand prints in the pavement and the outside of the clubs where the stars such as Frank Sinatra and Dean Martin sang looked very tatty. There were cheap shops all over the place selling mementos of old films and stars. We were certainly not impressed but perhaps this was due to the bad weather after the sunshine of Sydney.

It was not advisable to walk far in Los Angeles so we mainly used taxis to get around. If the weather had been nicer, I would have hired a car and perhaps visited Mexico but we decided against it in the conditions. There were floods everywhere and some of the roads were closed by landslides. Our days were spent wandering around the shopping Malls and eating at the various restaurants from all over the world. A trip to Santa Monica was also a bit of a disaster because of the rain so we spent the day again in the shopping Malls. Marie,s neck was still hurting and my ankle was playing up so we were both glad to get back to the hotel. We took another minibus trip around the town with a different driver and found it to be quite funny when he pointed out the houses where the stars lived at Bel Air which were completely different to the ones pointed out by the first driver, which one was the chancer, I don't know, probably both. It was a relief when the time came to go home. A ten and a half hour flight to Heathrow, a wait for a flight to Belfast, then home. It was a three month's holiday to remember but it was nice to arrive at Beechfield on Monday, 9th February, 1998, there is no place like home.

It was not long before I slipped back into the routine of golfing and the voluntary working as Secretary of both Mahee Golf Club and the Secretary Manager's Association. John McMillan acted for me in my absence at Mahee and things were running smoothly when I returned. I had been having some trouble with pain in my left ankle while walking. My doctor sent me to see Mr Simon Henderson, a surgeon at Musgrave Park Hospital and he told me they were considering replacing ankle bones and felt my ankle might be a useful case to consider. We took a couple more holidays during the year, a short break to the Royal Hotel in Bray and a trip to Portrush in April to the houses purchased by the Benevolent Society of the R.U.C. for holidays for police widows and pensioners. Later in June, we spent a fortnight in Florida on a fly drive holiday around the state, calling at Key West and up the East Coast to Orlando and down the West Coast again to Miami.

In September, Mr Henderson informed me that they were contemplating replacing my left ankle as a first in Northern Ireland and I was glad to consent. This operation had already been performed in Birmingham and Mr West came across from Birmingham Hospital and assisted by Mr Simon Henderson, performed a replacement ankle operation on me on 24th September, 1998. I remained in plaster until 19th October, when the plaster was removed. I felt the operation was a success as I have felt no pain in the ankle since. I received physiotherapy on the ankle for a couple of months to regain movement after the plaster was removed but the pain had gone and I was delighted with the result. Marie and I had a couple of days at the Regency

Hotel in Dublin in December and on Christmas Day we took my mother to the Millbrook Lodge for a meal.

1999 began with a National left handers golfing outing to Portmarnock and in March, Marie and I headed off for a fortnight to Florida which was becoming a favourite holiday destination, particularly because of the weather. My son Gary and I were now firm supporters of the Ulster Rugby team and had purchased stand tickets for all their home matches. I competed in the Irish Seniors Golf Tournament at Tullamore in June without success but on Captain's Day at Mahee, I was lucky enough to win Bobby Jellie's Captain's prize with a score of forty one points. I had a gross score of seventy two, the best score I have ever had.

Captain's Prize Winner 1998

A good mate, Alan Kennedy, also had a score of forty one points but I understand I only pipped him at the post on the last three holes. At the time, Alan was headmaster at Rathmore Primary School but he has now retired and like myself, enjoys his golf with the retired members who play every Wednesday. It was very much of a coincidence that when I obtained my fourth 'hole in one' at Mahee on Saturday, 28th June, 2008, Alan also has a 'hole in one' at the same hole on the same day.

In August, my brother Wallace and his wife Molly came across to Ireland for a visit and we had an enjoyable time together. Neil's father Duncan also visited and I played some golf with Neil and him at Mahee. In September, about twenty of us from Mahee travelled to what is known as Mervyn's weekend to Carlow. We played Mount Wolseley, Kilkea Castle and Rathsallagh golf Clubs. In November, my daughter Carol and her husband Billy went to Australia to visit her sister and we looked after their dog Jodie, a docile and lovable black Labrador. A quiet Christmas at home ended the year.

I still kept an interest in what was happening in the R.U.C. An independent commission on policing had been set up and its report was published in 1999 and among a number of recommendations, there were very few that the police did not already do, the one that annoyed me most was the re-naming of the Royal Ulster Constabulary to be the Police Service of Northern Ireland. I could understand that the R.U.C had been used in the past to bolster up the old Unionist regime in the North and again by the British Government against the Unionist Community but I was satisfied that the police service had changed sufficiently to being an impartial service in so far as that is possible in any human organisation. The buzz words in my time of service which were overused frequently were 'efficiency' and 'effectiveness'. I consider the present police service not to be independent of Government but to have been overtaken and controlled by a continually spreading civil service. It appears to try to operate the police service as a business, not a service to the public. The emphasis is on cost cutting and centralisation by closing stations and the public in small towns and rural areas are denied access to local police. Knowledge of local conditions and criminals has been lost to the police through this lack of daily contact. It was rewarding to receive the 'George Cross' as a member of the Royal Ulster Constabulary but it in no way compensates for the change of name of the police service I consider to have been the best in the world.

Had the Northern Ireland Community not been denied their franchise to vote for the main parties in the United Kingdom, perhaps they would have voted along real social issues and not sectarian issues and the last thirty years of conflict might have been avoided. I can understand there would always have been those who were intent on a United Ireland but surely this might have been pursued in a democratic way, rather than through terrorism. I have travelled a lot in the South of Ireland and find I probably have more in common with the Southern Irish than with the English. The British Government has a history of appeasement with terrorists. For example, negotiations in Cyprus and Israel where former terrorists in both countries took over the reins of power. My personal feelings are that the same now applies in Northern Ireland where we have been manipulated into being ruled by a minority Government comprising bigots of the D.U.P and former terrorists of Sinn Fein. I believe the majority in the North, Catholic and Protestant have difficulty in accepting the present arrangements but put up with them at present in the interests of peace following the I.R.A. cease-fire, only time will tell.

Enough of politics, in July of the millennium year, a number of guests attended the wedding of our son Gary at Carryduff Baptist Church and afterwards enjoyed the meal and dancing at La Mon House Hotel. The remainder of the year passed off quietly and in 2001, I was elected President of Mahee Island golf club for a two year period. By this time I had given up being Secretary and was replaced by Mervyn Marshall. I also retired as Secretary of N.I.S.M.A and was replaced by Dave Ryan, Bangor Golf Club. Marie and I still enjoyed our short break holidays to the South and to Portrush and began to go to Florida on a yearly basis. We were on a short break to Dublin in November when we were called back as Marie's oldest brother Eric was seriously ill. Eric sadly died after a short period and we attended the wake and funeral, another sad occasion. In January, 2002, we decided to take a winter break in the Canary Islands and in July, we moved house again to an apartment in central Bangor which would be more easily maintained. My President's Day took place in September and when my two years had finished, I decided to resign from Council at Mahee as I felt that I had done my time and fresh and younger ideas were required. In December, we had the unexpected pleasure of a visit from our daughter Valerie and husband Augustus from Australia but it was in sad circumstances as Augustus's mother, Maureen Edgar, had died and they were here for the funeral. It was nice though to have them for Christmas dinner, just like old times.

The New Year was welcomed in by Marie and I at the Regency Hotel in Dublin where we enjoyed a lovely meal and danced into 2003. In April we went to Majorca for an early holiday but found it too early as the weather was colder than expected. I travelled with the International Police Association Golfing Society to Scotland for a week's golf in May and we had a week in Portrush in June at the apartments of the Police Benevolent Society. I competed at the R.U.C. Society's Captain's Day at Donaghadee also in June and was lucky enough to win Jim Boyd's Captains Prize which was a lovely oil painting of the ninth hole at Royal County Down, it takes pride of place in my living room. Towards the end of June, we were informed that our grand-daughter Claire was getting married so we again set off for Australia for the wedding, via Singapore where we stayed for a couple of days. Our first stop in Australia was Brisbane in Queensland and we picked up the hired car and drove to Noosa Heads and to our pre-booked guest house, the "Outrigger". The weather was warm and sunny and in the evenings, we sat sipping wine on the balcony overlooking the Noosa river and around dusk, thousands of birds arrived in the trees opposite our balcony to settle in for the night. Their chattering made a terrific noise and all of a sudden when darkness fell, the noise stopped completely and there was complete silence. We enjoyed this phenomenon each evening.

We spent the second week at the Norfolk's Resort at Caloundra on the sunshine coast. The weather remained warm and sunny and following that we commenced the long drive to Sydney through Byron Bay, Ballina, Port Macquarie, Newcastle to Sydney, stopping for a night or two where necessary. We arrived in Sydney a couple of days before Claire's wedding which was to be held on 19th July. Claire was married in Wallace's church and it was a very nice occasion, a hymn written by my daughter Valerie was played at the service. The wedding ceremony was presided over by Wallace who in the evening performed as master of ceremonies at the wedding party at a nearby hotel. The weather in Sydney was noticeably colder than in Queensland and in fact I noticed frost on the ground on one or two occasions. It warmed up during the daylight hours bust cooled considerably at night.

The next couple of weeks were spent in sight-seeing around Sydney and Darling Harbour, visiting places such as Katoomba, Kiami and Camden market. Our socialising was in the Revesby Rugby League Club where we went most evenings for a meal and entertainment. The time to leave again came around too quickly and we headed off in Wallace's bus for the airport. We said our goodbyes and boarded the flight to Singapore where we stayed for two days before catching the flight to London. The London flight took twelve hours, thirty-five minutes and was rather bumpy as we passed over Thailand. As usual, when we arrived in Belfast, we were glad to be home after such a long and tiring journey. Marie and I then looked after her sister Margaret's dogs in Comber for a couple of weeks while she was on holidays and later we looked after our daughter Carol's dog for a fortnight. We spent a week in Blackpool in September and in October, I bought myself a motor cycle, a 600cc Suzuki GSXF which I enjoyed riding around the Ards peninsula. In retrospect, quite a lot had been packed into the year 2003.

We took our usual two day break to the Regency Hotel in Dublin in February, 2004 and stayed at the Portrush Apartments in March. My son Gary had purchased a black labrador called Bud and as both he and Lynn were working, Marie and I walked a lot every day, we often took Bud with us on walks along the shore at Cloughy. He enjoyed the open spaces. In April, we celebrated my daughter Gwen's and husband Neil's 25th wedding anniversary with a beautiful meal in Coyle's restaurant in Bangor. In May, I travelled again with the I.P.A's Golfing Society to Scotland for our annual trip and played Hilton Park, Vale of Leven, Shaws Park, Callender and Beigh Golf Clubs. We spent the last fortnight in May at Carol's house while she and Billy were on holidays. Early in June, my brother Wallace and Molly visited from Australia and then we spent some time in Comber at Margaret's while she and Jim were on holidays.

In September, I booked a holiday in Florida, first to New Smyrna Beach, then to a villa near Orlando. This turned out to be quite eventful in that while we were in the hotel block, a hurricane was forecast approaching from the South. There appeared to be quite a panic as people began boarding up windows and traffic was already building up on the highways, evacuating north towards Jacksonville and South Carolina. I asked one of the waitresses why and she informed me that she was also going to evacuate that evening. On her say so, we decided also to move out of the hotel and drove north, finally finishing up in Georgia. We spent a couple of days there as the storm swept through Florida then decided we would ring our next door neighbour beside our hired villa to find out what was happening. It turned out that there were no shops or filling stations closed which had been forecast and damage was minimal. We drove back to Orlando and to the villa where we found everything in order. We could have been there much sooner. However, our future yearly trips to Florida were booked for early in the year, away from the hurricane season. In December, Carol and Billy moved to a new house near Ballywalter and we assisted with the move and on Christmas Day, we had dinner at the Millbrook Lodge Hotel with my mother.

Holiday in 2005 began with a short two day break to the Royal Hotel in Brae. In February, we were walking along the beach in Cloughy with Gary's dog Bud when my mobile phone rang. Gary told us that his wife Lynn had just had a baby boy and we both delighted. We went to the hospital as soon as possible and I had my photograph taken with my newest (eighth) grandchild who was later to be named after me. Although this was not my first male grandson, he is the one who will carry the Reid name into the future. Carol and Billy went away in April and we stayed in their house which was almost a holiday in itself. In early May we had the pleasure of attending our first grandaughter, Natasha's wedding in Bangor and we dressed up in our best suits for a wonderful day, both at St Bernadettes Chapel and the reception later at Clandeboye Lodge Hotel. We enjoyed the villa in Florida so much, I booked it again and we headed off later in May after Natasha's wedding and before the hurricane season. The villa belongs to a police colleague, Seamus McBride and has four bedrooms with a swimming pool. It was very relaxing to go out for groceries, then lie by the pool in the beautiful sunshine, with no interruptions. We had already visited Disney World and the Film Studios a number of times so we spent most of our time just walking, swimming and relaxing. In June, we took our usual week to the apartments in Portrush and stayed at Margaret's while she was on holidays. I began a course in digital photography at Bangor College and managed to obtain a City & Guilds Certificate.

I was still very much involved with golf, playing every Saturday and also with the various societies of which I was a member.

Our Saturday fourball had changed, in that John Marshall senior stopped playing because of a troublesome knee and young John began to play in the afternoons. Tommy Murphy has stopped playing on a Saturday and Gary Montgomery took over from John junior. Davy Andrews unfortunately passed away recently and Dicky Simpson and Allen Garrett have joined the present fourball. The competition for a pound is still closely contested. Friday or Saturday evenings were spent at Ravenhill when the Ulster Rugby team were competing and Gary and I enjoyed the excitement and atmosphere, especially when Ulster was winning and doing well. We had Christmas dinner at Gary,s and finished the year off by booking into the Royal Hotel at Bray for the New Year's Eve party. A quieter but very enjoyable year.

We were glad to be involved in occasional days of my grandson Tom's early years and we got great pleasure in looking after him now and again. Formative years pass so quickly and we took great pleasure from watching his progress. 2006 began with Carol and Billy taking a short break in February and we looked after the house for a few days. Gary moved house in April from Newtownards to Groomsport and I again arranged a holiday in Florida in May to the villa in Davenport, near Orlando. We were informed by Valerie that her son, my grandson Daniel, was also getting married so this meant another trip to Australia at the end of June into July. Unfortunately, it was winter in Australia but we did the usual stop-over in Singapore where it is always warm so we experienced some good weather. On this occasion, Daniel's wedding was scheduled for 8th July so this time I arranged for Valerie and Augustus to accompany Marie and I after the wedding, to spend a week with us at Norfolks Resort, Moffats Beach in Caloundra where we had such a good time on our previous visit. We stopped in Singapore for a couple of days on our return to break the journey and arrived home in early August.

Margaret went on holidays in August so we went to Comber to look after the pets for a fortnight. Later in August, I went with the P.S.N.I. Senior Officers Golf Section to play the Garda at Westmanstown. Tommy Murphy also came along as my guest and we had an excellent day out followed by a great dinner and entertainment. We had played in a similar competition at Portadown the previous year and were able to renew old acquaintances. Marie and I spent a week at Gary's house to let them away for a holiday, and by this time we at Mahee together with Carnalea Golf Club initiated and joined a veterans' golf league involving six teams Mahee, Carnalea, Mount Ober, Rockmount, Kirkiston Castle and Ormeau. Each team plays each other home and away and the home team stands the visiting team their meal. It works very successfully and there is a finals day at each of the clubs in rotation. I looked after the team for the first couple of years then handed over the reins to Leslie Emmett. Leslie has since passed it on to Trevor Geddis who holds the reins at present. Mervyn Marshalls' week-end took place that year in Tullamore where we stayed at the Bridge Hotel. Gary and I still had season tickets for the Ulster Rugby at Ravenhill and enjoyed all Magner's league and European home matches throughout the winter and travelled to Lansdowne Road in Dublin on the odd occasion to watch the International matches. Christmas dinner was enjoyed at Gary's in Groomsport.

The rugby highlight in early in 2007 was the match between Ireland and England which Ireland won by forty three points to thirteen. Dublin was awash with Irish and English colours and the atmosphere at Lansdowne Road was electric. Celebrations went on into the night and Gary and I stopped at a road-side hotel for dinner on the way home. The restaurant was buzzing and everyone flushed with success. Marie and I had enjoyed our Florida holiday to the villa so much that I booked it again for May and we spent three glorious weeks. Our usual pilgrimage to Portrush took place for a week in June and we let Margaret and Jim away for a holiday by looking after the pets. The week-end away with the Mahee golfers took place in September to Co Meath and following that we attended our granddaughter Carly's wedding at the Abbey Church in Bangor. Our other grand-daughter Trudy was married the following month and we had a great time at the wedding and reception afterwards at the Old Inn, Crawfordsburn. I had been having some difficulty with my eyesight and my optician thought it could be helped by surgery. He notified my doctor and I was called to Ards Hospital to see a specialist. I was told there was a process of lens replacement which would probably help my sight and in the middle of November, I was called to Lagan Valley Hospital to have the necessary surgery. This was done firstly on my right eye with outstanding success. I was amazed at the difference in sight and appreciated the colours around me.

Marie's seventieth birthday was due in November so I thought I would spring a surprise on her. I arranged for our eldest daughter Valerie and husband Augustus to travel from Australia and booked a party at Tullyglass House Hotel for the occasion with the rest of the family. Marie was unaware that Valerie had arrived until she phoned her mum as if from Australia, then just walked in. Marie almost fainted but when she recovered, was delighted she had the complete family together. It was a nice end to an eventful year.

We booked our usual holiday for the incoming year in Florida but on this occasion, we booked three weeks, April into May and Gary and Tom accompanied us for the first week. We had a great time but missed them when they returned home. I went with the I.P.A. Golf Society to Rosyth in Scotland for a week which revived fond memories of the years of banter from the late Davy McKirgan and the late Robin Walker who were no longer with us. June saw us again to the apartments at Portrush and later in Comber for two weeks with Margaret's pets. By this time, I had surgery on my other eye and my sight was unbelievable, having used glasses for many years, I could see clearly without them and only needed them for small print. In August, Marie and I spent a couple of days at the Regency Hotel in Dublin and in September

I went to Carlow on our usual golfing week-end from Mahee. We spent a quiet Christmas dinner at home with the family.

The present year has followed on very much like the others since I retired. However, we had a worrying time in February and early March. My brother Harry was suffering from chest pains and had been diagnosed with coronary artery decease. He was scheduled for a by pass operation in Dublin and Marie and I visited him and Jean shortly after the operation. He was up and walking about, obviously drugged so soon after a quadruple by-pass that I was concerned for his safety and when he returned home, a long journey from Dublin to Bangor in about a week, he was so ill he had to be taken immediately to the Ulster Hospital. At that time I feared for his life. I'm delighted and relieved to say that he has recovered well and back to his normal self. The last few years of my retirement probably sounds repetitive and boring but I must say my life is anything but boring. I cannot believe that it is almost nineteen years since I left the R.U.C. Marie and I enjoy our walk every day, we enjoy our short holidays to the South of Ireland and to Florida where we were again in May, I enjoy my weekly golf and my music on keyboard and accordion.

The highlight of the year was my mother's ninetieth birthday. We held a party with all the family at Tullyglass House Hotel, Ballymena. Wallace and Molly and Valerie and Augustus came from Australia for the special event. She had a great time with all her children and grand-children present. Marie and I enjoyed a trip to Scotland recently on a Highland Heritage tour and were delighted to meet former colleagues who were also present. I attended a P.S.N.I. / R.U.C. Senior Officers dinner at Newforge where I had the opportunity to meet many of the officers I had served with over the past fifty years and able to recall memories and discuss the good and troubled times of the past. It also brought to mind those officers who gave their lives for the people of this province.

Chapter 12
(Epilogue)

Why did I write this book? I have read many articles about policing, politics and troubles but I feel the story of the ordinary policeman has not been told. I am from a working class background, lucky enough to have a solid up-bringing in a good family and had the opportunity to join a police service of which I am very proud. The views expressed in this biography are my own and I take full responsibility and apologise for any errors or omissions I may have made. I found the great majority of members of the Royal Ulster Constabulary, Protestant and Catholic, to be responsible, highly motivated individuals. I worked with men and women who donned their uniform daily, making them easily identifiable, who faced danger in difficult areas without question, when they knew that gunmen and murderers were skulking and hiding and using the population as a shield. This was not a four month tour but over a period of many years, day after day, and I have nothing but admiration for each of them. I have seen them answer calls, many of which were hoax or ambush calls without hesitation as they did their duty. I attended many of their funerals and seen horrific injuries as a result of this bravery. Society will never repay those officers for their dedication and service.

It is ironic that those arguing at present about the transfer of policing and justice to local government from the mother Parliament, are the very people whose supporters in society continually flouted the law in the past. I do not have respect for a number of politicians, many of whom have claimed excess expenses at a cost to the tax payer. The power sharing executive in the early seventies had a chance as it was composed mainly of middle ground politicians from both sides but unfortunately, those in power in Northern Ireland today, the extremes, were pushed into their positions because of their belligerence.

Society has changed considerably in my lifetime, in the forties and fifties, a crime such as murder was unusual and might happen once a year, at present it is almost a weekly occurrence. Minority pressure groups are vociferous and Christian values and morals are under constant attack. Single person families are the norm and mis.interpreted equality laws which argue that women and men are the same, are causing young women to lose their femininity as they try to compete with the behaviour of their male counterparts. Feminism and Gay rights are the buzz words. Family is under attack and extended family support is under pressure. Rules and regulations around health and safety initiated from Europe are changing parental responsibility and children now dictate to parents as to how they should be brought up. Sincere people who might work to improve the well- being of children are put off by the number of regulations and checks regarding child abuse.

As I write, Republicans, albeit dissident republicans, continue to murder British soldiers and endeavour to murder police, their own country-men. Those Republicans in Government know who they are and I await in anticipation their re-action, before I judge them. I will not hold my breath. I have met and have friends in golfing circles who hold republican views which I respect, but now is the time for action to halt terrorism in Ireland once and for all.

Enough ranting, I have had a very fruitful and happy life. The person mainly responsible for it is my wife Marie. She has managed to keep me on the right path when at times it looked as if I might slip off. She is the love of my life and I am proud of my children, the girls, Valerie, Gwendoline and Carol, and Gary who still serves in the P.S.N.I., They gave us eight wonderful grandchildren who in turn have given us eight great grandchildren. My grand daughter Natasha also serves in the P.S.N.I and so continues a long tradition of family service as does my eldest grandson Jonathan, now a Corporal in the British Army. I have a full life including the pleasure of being made an honorary member of my golf club. Marie and I have reasonable health, walk every day and enjoy our holidays. I enjoy my Golf, Music, watching Rugby and Football and have the company of many good friends in the world of police, golf and music. My plans for the future are to continue to enjoy my golf, make C.D's. of my music, watch our newest and youngest grandson Tom develop and perhaps think of another book.

I hope the situation will improve for the people of Northern Ireland as all have suffered greatly over the past forty years. The P.S.N.I. have my best wishes but I feel the cutting back of Police Reserve, and the centralisation policy of closing rural stations continues to move the police away from people and local knowledge and friendship essential for good policing is lost. I am eternally grateful to the R.U.C. for giving me self esteem loyalty and comradeship over many years and into retirement. When I see what has happened in Government over the past few years I feel I have something in common with Margaret Thatcher and Ian Paisley in that I have learned in my lifetime and I hope they also have learned is that one should 'never say never'.

The Award of the George Cross to the Royal Ulster Constabulary

Citation:

"For the past 30 years, the Royal Ulster Constabulary has been the bulwark against, and the main target of, a sustained and brutal terrorism campaign. The Force has suffered heavily in protecting both sides of the community from danger - 302 officers have been killed in the line of duty and thousands more have been injured, many seriously. Many officers have been ostracised by their own community and others have been forced to leave their homes in the face of threats to them and their families.

As Northern Ireland reaches a turning point in its political development this award is made to recognise the collective courage and dedication to duty of all of those who have served in the Royal Ulster Constabulary and who have accepted the danger and stress this has brought to them and their families".

Buckingham Palace, 23rd November 1999

Acknowledgements

1. My son Gary - thanks for help and suggestions

2. Alan Kennedy - thanks for help in assisting with proof reading.

3. Dennis Nash - thanks for advice and help with photographs.

4. Wesley Johnston - thanks for patience and input.